Number Works!

HOMEWORK BOOK

Graham Newman

Stanley Thornes (Publishers) Ltd

First published in 2000 by:

Nelson Thornes
Delta Place
27 Bath Road
Cheltenham
Glos GL53 7TH

00 01 02 03 04 / 10 9 8 7 6 5 4 3 2 1

A catalogue record of this book is available from the British Library

ISBN 0 7487 5449 0

Typeset by Florence Production Limited
Printed and bound in Great Britain by Redwood Books, Trowbridge, Wiltshire.

Contents

Introduction

The *Number Works!* books have been written to support work in numeracy. This skill has many applications and can be developed through formal "taught" lessons and support sessions, as well as outside the school environment.

The *Number Works!* core book is for pupils to use mainly within lessons, either during school time or as part of an after-school club or Summer Numeracy School.

The *Number Works!* homework book is for pupils to use for homework to support the work in the core book, or for parents and helpers to use either at home or in out-of-hours school sessions. This could also be in preparation, or as follow up work, for a Summer Numeracy School.

Although the homework book can be used alone, it is linked to and supports the core book. The answer section for each chapter begins with a table showing how the sections in the two books are linked. Thus after working on a section in the core book, pupils can be set the corresponding exercise in the homework book.

Parents and helpers boxes suggest hints and methods for completing problems, and also suggest activities for further practice, where appropriate. At the end of each chapter Activities provide pupils with opportunities to strengthen their numeracy skills through games, puzzles and investigations.

The work is differentiated throughout, starting with simpler tasks and progressing on to more difficult aspects of numeracy. There are answers to all the exercises in the back of the book.

Number Works! does not aim to be exhaustive. Everyday life itself provides a wealth of uses of numeracy, and confidence in numeracy skills is essential. This book supports all those wishing to improve these skills.

Graham Newman

1 Number

1 Place value

Many foreign currencies have notes and coins that show a clear place value.
These are Spanish pesetas:

2×1000 3×100 6×10 5×1
$= 2000$ $= 300$ $= 60$ $= 5$

```
2000
 300
  60
   5
─────
2365  pesetas
```

Exercise 1:1

Find the total amounts.

1

_____ pesetas

2

_____ pesetas

3

_____ pesetas

4

_____ pesetas

5

_____ pesetas

6  _____ pesetas

7  _____ pesetas

8  _____ pesetas

2   Numbers to words

In large numbers the digits can be grouped together.

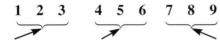

To write 4 1 0 2 0 4 2 in words, group the digits together.
Split them into threes, starting at the right hand end:

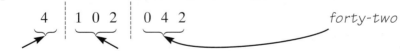

The number is four million, one hundred and two thousand, and forty-two.

Exercise 1:2

Write these numbers in words.

1   4137

_____

2   3584

_____

3   8061

_____

4   4370

_____

5   6060

_____

6   32 780

_____

7   97 542

_____

8   630 381

_____

9   175 060

_____

10   234 024

_____

11   3 042 510

_____

12   12 403 519

_____

ACTIVITY

Read out your answers to someone.
Ask them to write the answer down as a number.
Do they get the number that you started with?

3   Words to numbers

When numbers are written in words, or spoken out loud, you can divide them up to help you write them in figures.

this means the end of the thousands

One hundred and four thousand | three hundred and ten

1 0 4   3 1 0

This number is 104 310

Exercise 1:3

Write these numbers in figures.

1   Two thousand seven hundred and forty-five   _____

2   Seven thousand six hundred and four   _____

3   Four thousand and three   _____

4   Sixty-five thousand eight hundred and forty   _____

5   Fifty-four thousand two hundred and three   _____

6 Forty thousand seven hundred and thirteen _____

7 Eighty-three thousand four hundred and thirty-six _____

8 One hundred and three thousand four hundred and twenty _____

9 Five hundred thousand four hundred and fifty _____

10 Two hundred and ninety-five thousand and fourteen _____

11 One million, three hundred and twenty thousand, four hundred and ninety _____

12 Fourteen million, three hundred thousand and twenty _____

PARENTS AND HELPERS

Everyone needs practice at writing down numbers. For this exercise you could read out these numbers to be written down.

For more practice, read out other numbers of a similar size.

4 Ordering numbers

The greater the **value** of a digit, the more important or **significant** it is.

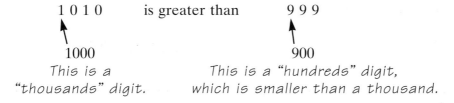

To write numbers in **descending** order start with the largest.
To write numbers in **ascending** order start with the smallest.

EXAMPLE

Write in descending order:

5421,   5820,   6402,   987,   5450

Look at the most significant digits first.

5421,   5820,   6402,   987,   5450   *largest number to the front*

6402,   5421,   5820,   987,   5450   *largest of all that start with 5*
6402,   5820,   5421,   987,   5450   *Next largest of all that start with 5*
6402,   5820,   5450,   5421,   987   *Done!*

Exercise 1:4

Write these numbers in **descending** order:

1   2654, 3857, 1994, 2451

2   7033, 7100, 6900, 6804

3   4005, 3981, 3750, 4200

4   890, 821, 848, 843

5   6547, 18 421, 17 453, 18 851

6   54 300, 51 207, 48 543, 65 217

Write these numbers in **ascending** order:

7   486, 478, 426, 295

8   300, 289, 303, 274

9   631, 422, 313, 622, 544

10   750, 731, 787, 763

11   318, 581, 268, 142, 99

12   5421, 5563, 5827, 5423

PARENTS AND HELPERS

Practise ordering at home by sorting the shopping into order by price/cost.

Then order by size and weight: the order will not be the same!

5   Less than or equal to

All these signs mean different things:

>	⩾	⩽	<
greater than	**greater than or equal to**	**less than or equal to**	**less than**
4 > 3	=	0 < 2	
4 is greater than 3	equal to	0 is less than 2	

Which signs will you put between the numbers?

> ⩾ = ⩽ <

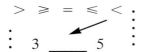
3 _____ 5

> ⩾ = ⩽ <

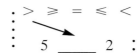
5 _____ 2

EXAMPLE

Circle all the numbers that are ⩾ 4:

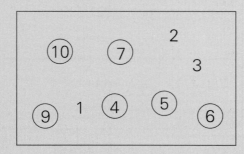

Exercise 1:5

Write the correct sign between each pair of numbers:

1 3 _____ 3   **2** 4 _____ 1   **3** 5 _____ 8   **4** 2 _____ 5

5 8 _____ 3   **6** 1 _____ 7   **7** 9 _____ 9   **8** 6 _____ 2

9 7 _____ 7   **10** 8 _____ 4   **11** 5 _____ 5   **12** 3 _____ 6

Circle the numbers in the rectangle to show less than or greater than.

13

1		2
3	4	9
	7	8

≤ 3

14

	2	4
5	6	9
	7	

< 14

15

2	3	6
5	7	9
	4	

≥ 6

16

8	2	5
	7	3
1	9	

≥ 7

17

2	3	
	7	4
6	9	1

≤ 4

18

5	6	1
9	4	
	2	7

> 5

6 Number lines

```
0   1   2   3   4   5   6   7   8   9
```

This is a number line.

When we want to show <4, that **does not** include the 4.
We draw it like this:

```
0   1   2   3   4   5   6   7   8   9
━━━━━━━━━━━━━○
```

When we want to show ≥6, that **does** include the 6.
We draw it like this:

```
0   1   2   3   4   5   6   7   8   9
                    ●━━━━━━━━
```

Exercise 1:6

Write down what these number lines show:

1
```
0   1   2   3   4   5   6   7   8   9
                        ○━━━━
```
_____

2
```
0   1   2   3   4   5   6   7   8   9
━━━━━━━━━━━━━━━━━━━●
```
_____

3
```
0   1   2   3   4   5   6   7   8   9
━━━━━━━━━━━━●
```
_____

4
```
0   1   2   3   4   5   6   7   8   9
            ●━━━━━━━━━━━━
```
_____

5
```
0   1   2   3   4   5   6   7   8   9
━━━━━━━━━━○
```
_____

6
```
0   1   2   3   4   5   6   7   8   9
        ●━━━━━━━━━━━━━━━━
```
_____

7
```
0   1   2   3   4   5   6   7   8   9
                ●━━━━━━━━━
```
_____

8
```
0   1   2   3   4   5   6   7   8   9
━━━━━━━━━━━━━━━━━━○
```
_____

Draw on each number line to show these:

9   0 1 2 3 4 5 6 7 8 9
                    ≤1

10   0 1 2 3 4 5 6 7 8 9
                       >4

11   0 1 2 3 4 5 6 7 8 9
                     >8

12   0 1 2 3 4 5 6 7 8 9
                       ≤3

13   0 1 2 3 4 5 6 7 8 9
                     ≥2

14   0 1 2 3 4 5 6 7 8 9
                       <5

15   0 1 2 3 4 5 6 7 8 9
                     <4

16   0 1 2 3 4 5 6 7 8 9
                       ≥6

7   Estimating numbers

Look at each of the cards shown.
Do not count the dots shown, but quickly try to guess how many there are on
each card.

 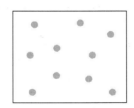  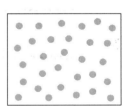

Now count the dots. How accurate were your estimates?

Exercise 1:7

Do not count the dots.
Quickly try to guess how many there are on each card.

1

2

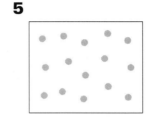

3

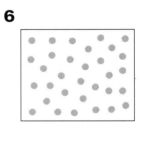

_____

_____

_____

4

5

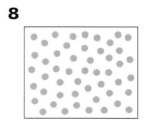

6

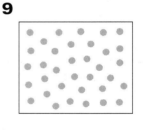

_____

_____

_____

7

8

9

_____

_____

_____

PARENTS AND HELPERS

You can make a game of estimation.

You need a collection of marbles, counters, or other smaller objects.

Player 1 sets out any number of counters between 10 and 20.

Player 2 looks at them for 5 seconds and estimates how many there are.

Score 1 penalty point for each incorrect counter guessed. For example, if there are 10 counters and you guess 8, score 2 penalty points.

Player 2 now sets out counters for player 1 to guess.

After 5 turns each, the winner is the player with the fewest penalty points.

8 Writing money

When writing money you need to make sure you write exactly **two** figures for the pence.

£ 3 . 2 1

Pounds — *Pence up to 99p (two figures)*
Remember 100p = £1

Sometimes a calculator shows an amount of money incorrectly:

4.2

You should write it using correct money notation: £ 4 . 2 **0**

Add the 0 to make two figures for the pence.

Exercise 1:8

These calculator displays show amounts of money.
Write them using correct money notation.

1	2	3	4
7.5	3.3	18.7	20.9
£ ______	£ ______	£ ______	£ ______

5	6	7	8
87.1	244.5	8.4	6.
£ ______	£ ______	£ ______	£ ______

Use a calculator to add up these amounts of money.
Write the answer using correct money notation.

9   £1.53 + £3.17

£_____

10   £5.21 + £13.49

£_____

11   £6.44 + £2.76

£_____

12   £18.75 + £26.65

£_____

13   £14.38 + £39.82

£_____

14   £13.47 + £24.53

£_____

Note: the correct way of writing three pounds and twenty-one pence is £3.21, but it has become acceptable (though it is strictly incorrect) to write it as £3.21p.
It is completely wrong to write it as 3.21p.

9   Rounding numbers

To the nearest 10

The numbers 161, 162, 163, 164 are all nearer 160 than 170, and are rounded to 160.

The numbers 166, 167, 168, 169 are all nearer 170 than 160, and are rounded to 170.

The number 165 is exactly halfway between 160 and 170.

Numbers halfway are normally rounded **up**, so 165 is rounded to 170.

To the nearest 100

All the numbers 401 up to 449 are nearer to 400 than 500, and are rounded to 400.

All the numbers 451 up to 499 are nearer to 500 than 400, and are rounded to 500.

The number 450 is exactly halfway between 400 and 500.

Numbers halfway are normally rounded **up**, so 450 is rounded to 500.

To the nearest 1000

Numbers are rounded to the nearest 1000 in the same way.

3500 is rounded **up** to 4000.

Exercise 1:9

Round to the nearest 10:

1	74	**2**	23	**3**	58	**4**	37	**5**	91

6	45	**7**	382	**8**	549	**9**	65	**10**	116

Round to the nearest 100:

11	261	**12**	818	**13**	534	**14**	976	**15**	850

16	625	**17**	2489	**18**	253	**19**	1397	**20**	742

Round to the nearest 1000:

21	5373	**22**	8438	**23**	1254	**24**	6055	**25**	7127

1 The disco

A number of people went to a disco.
Martin, the doorman, says that about 60 people went in,
but he can't remember exactly how many.

50 51 52 53 54 55 56 57 58 59

60 61 62 63 64 65 66 67 68 69

Circle any of these numbers that give 60 when rounded
to the nearest 10.

What is the smallest number that rounds off to give 60?

————————

What is the largest number that rounds off to give 60?

————————

2 The numbers game

a Start with a number (say 4).

b Choose a target number less than 100 (say 35).

c Write down at least three different ways you can get from your starting
number to your target number.

For example:

$4 \times 10 - 5 = 35$ $\qquad$ $4 \times 8 + 3 = 35$ $\qquad$ $(4+3) \times 5 = 35$

Try this game with different starting numbers and different target numbers.

Starting number	Target number	Three ways
————	————	—————————————————
————	————	—————————————————
————	————	—————————————————
————	————	—————————————————
————	————	—————————————————
————	————	—————————————————

2 Addition

1 Addition with carries

We get carries when we have to "carry" a number over in a sum:

$$
\begin{array}{r}
4\ 7 \\
+\ 1\ 6 \\
\hline
\end{array}
\qquad
\begin{array}{r}
7 \\
+\ 6 \\
\hline
1\ 3
\end{array}
$$

You have a carry!

The first or carry digit goes here

$$
4 + 1 + \textcircled{1} = 6
\qquad
\begin{array}{r}
4\ \diagup 7 \\
+\ 1\,_1\ 6 \\
\hline
6\ 3
\end{array}
$$

The second digit goes here.

Exercise 2:1

Work out these addition sums.
Which questions have carry numbers?

1
$$
\begin{array}{r}
6\ 2 \\
+\ 1\ 5 \\
\hline
\end{array}
$$

2
$$
\begin{array}{r}
5\ 4 \\
+\ 2\ 3 \\
\hline
\end{array}
$$

3
$$
\begin{array}{r}
1\ 4\ 4 \\
+\ \ \ 3\ 5 \\
\hline
\end{array}
$$

4
$$
\begin{array}{r}
5\ 6 \\
+\ 3\ 7 \\
\hline
\end{array}
$$

5
$$
\begin{array}{r}
4\ 3\ 7 \\
+\ \ \ 6\ 1 \\
\hline
\end{array}
$$

6
$$
\begin{array}{r}
3\ 8 \\
+\ 5\ 4 \\
\hline
\end{array}
$$

7
$$
\begin{array}{r}
1\ 6\ 4 \\
+\ 3\ 8\ 4 \\
\hline
\end{array}
$$

8
$$
\begin{array}{r}
3\ 0\ 2 \\
+\ 6\ 9\ 7 \\
\hline
\end{array}
$$

9
$$
\begin{array}{r}
3\ 7 \\
+\ 4\ 7 \\
\hline
\end{array}
$$

10
$$
\begin{array}{r}
3\ 4\ 7 \\
+\ 6\ 5\ 2 \\
\hline
\end{array}
$$

11
$$
\begin{array}{r}
9\ 3 \\
+\ 1\ 6 \\
\hline
\end{array}
$$

12
$$
\begin{array}{r}
7\ 7\ 7 \\
+\ 2\ 1\ 3 \\
\hline
\end{array}
$$

13 $1423 + 645$

14 $223 + 484$

15 $624 + 547$

2 Addition with several carries

With several carries you need to keep your work clear and organised.
You need to see clearly where the carries are to be added.
Make sure you keep your work in neat columns.

```
  H T U
  8 7 8
+ 5 6 9
─────────
```
Do the sum in three stages:
Units → Tens → Hundreds

```
  H  T  U             H  T  U             H  T  U
  8  7  8             8  7  8             8  7  8
  5  7₁ 9      →      5₁ 7₁ 9      →      5₁ 7₁ 9
────────            ────────            ────────
      7                  5  7            1  4  5  7
```

Carry from units. *Carry from tens.* *Write down the full number in the answer line.*

Exercise 2:2

Work out these addition sums.

1
```
  3 2 1 3
+ 1 9 0 8
─────────
```

2
```
  1 2 3
+ 3 2 1
───────
```

3
```
  4 5 5
+ 6 0 6
───────
```

4
```
  9 6 8
+ 7 7 7
───────
```

5
```
  7 0 9
+ 5 0 6
───────
```

6
```
  1 4 0 6
+    8 0 7
─────────
```

7
```
  2 8 3 8
+ 2 8 0 4
─────────
```

8
```
  8 4 4 2
+ 4 1 5 6
─────────
```

9
```
    3 2 1
+ 4 7 0 9
─────────
```

10
```
  9 0 7 5
+ 2 0 8 6
─────────
```

11
```
  3 8 4 7
+ 5 2 8 4
─────────
```

12
```
  5 6 4 8
+ 1 6 5 6
─────────
```

13 4017 + 1645

14 8348 + 1937

15 7657 + 4309

3 Lining up

When you write out a sum, make sure you line up the figures on the right hand side.

$$34 + 231 \longrightarrow \begin{array}{r} 3\ 4 \\ +\ \underline{2\ 3\ 1} \\ 2\ 6\ 5 \end{array}$$ *Line up here*

Stop

$$3415 + 21 \longrightarrow \begin{array}{r} 3\ 4\ 1\ 5 \\ +\ \underline{2\ 1} \\ 3\ 4\ 3\ 6 \end{array}$$

Exercise 2:3

Do these addition sums.
Write out each sum and *line those figures up!*

1 484 + 15

2 219 + 19

3 1004 + 342

4 1437 + 28

5 2418 + 674

6 1034 + 99

7 487 + 1905

8 68 + 1596

9 Asha had £2088 in her bank account.
She put another £65 in the bank.
How much is in her bank account now? _____

10 Sean has a collection of 183 stamps.
He buys another 39 stamps.
How many stamps does Sean have now? _____

4   Adding money

When you line up the figures in a money sum, you need to keep the pounds and the pence separate:

$£6 + £4.32 + 56p \longrightarrow$

```
     £   p
     6        ←——— Put £ in the £ column.
     4.32
 +     56     ←——— Put amounts in pence
 ————————           in the pence column.
 £  10.88
```

Exercise 2:4

Add up these amounts of money.
Write down the answer using correct money notation.

1   £3.21 + 46p

2   £4.21 + 39p

3   £3.34 + £7

4   28p + £3.84

5   £6 + £5.80

6   85p + £4.73

7   £1.10 + 68p + £4.77

8   83p + 47p + 75p

9   £6 + £3.30 + £5

10   £4.92 + 80p + £8

11   92p + £1.40 + 67p

12   £7 + £14.50 + 70p

13 £5.88 + £9 + 10p

14 75p + 16p + £1.16

15 40p + £1.80 + £7

16 65p + £2.85 + 97p

5 Adding mentally

Exercise 2:5

Add these numbers up in your head.
Write down the answer only, unless you get completely stuck!

1

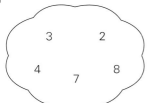

2

3

4

5

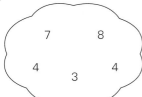

6

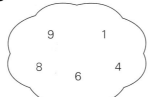

7

4 7

8 5

3

_____

8

9 4

6 8

5

_____

9

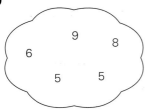

9

6 8

5 5

_____

10

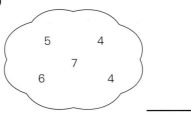

5 4

7

6 4

_____

11

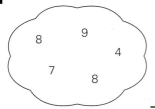

8 9

4

7

8

_____

12

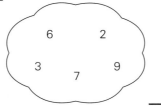

6 2

3 9

7

_____

6   Mental calculation

You may have larger numbers to add up mentally.
Add the units and the tens separately.

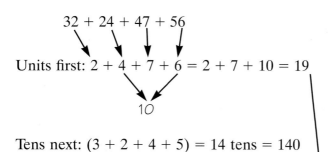

$$32 + 24 + 47 + 56$$

Units first: $2 + 4 + 7 + 6 = 2 + 7 + 10 = 19$

10

Tens next: $(3 + 2 + 4 + 5) = 14$ tens $= 140$

Total: $140 + 19 = 159$

Exercise 2:6

Add these numbers up in your head.
Write down the answer only, unless you get completely stuck!

1 53 + 17 + 43   **2** 27 + 38 + 33   **3** 27 + 38 + 35

_____   _____   _____

4 43 + 48 + 34   **5** 28 + 33 + 64   **6** 30 + 45 + 25

_____   _____   _____

7 46 + 37 + 26 + 17   **8** 38 + 37 + 52

_____   _____

9 40 + 53 + 29 + 27   **10** 36 + 15 + 56 + 30

_____   _____

11 58 + 13 + 37 + 18   **12** 59 + 32 + 18 + 38

_____   _____

13 Penny is playing darts.
With her three darts she scores
39, 18 and 36.
What is her total score?

14 Four adults were playing a double
game of tennis.
Their ages were 48, 46, 39 and 52.
What was their total age?

_____

15 Four coaches are needed for
a school trip.
The numbers of pupils on each
coach are 53, 47, 45 and 56.
What is the total number of pupils
on the trip?

_____

K9 the robot dog

K9 the robot dog likes adding up so much –
you can't stop him!

He added up the counting numbers: 1 + 2
1 + 2 + 3
1 + 2 + 3 + 4
. . .

and found the answers: 3, 6, 10, . . .

How far can you go? Add up all the numbers up to 20.

K9 adds up all the **even** numbers: 2 + 4 + 6 + 8 + . . .

What can you get to?
What do these numbers and the answers have in common?

K9 adds up all the **odd** numbers: 1 + 3 + 5 + 7 + . . .

What can you get to?
What do these numbers and the answers have in common?

PARENTS AND HELPERS

You need to practise adding up together.
Regular practice will improve this skill.
There is an adding up table on page 163 to
use for this practice. Read out two numbers
to be added, and you can read off the
answer from the table.

Remember a well answered practice session,
and good progress, deserves a reward!

Another way to practise numeracy is either
to add up the amounts spend on goods
bought when shopping, or to count amounts
of money at home.

This example shows how adding up can be
used to calculate change:

EXAMPLE

To find the change from
£10 for £9.49

£ 9.49
+   1p
£ 9.50
+   50p
£10.00

Change: 1p + 50p = 51p

3 Subtraction

1 Subtraction without borrowing

You can use two methods to find the **difference** between numbers.

Work out $79 - 43$

To find $9 - 3$:

Method 1: take away

Count down from 9:

9 8 7 6 5 4 3

6 numbers down

so $9 - 3 = 6$

Method 2: adding

Count up from 9:

3 4 5 6 7 8 9

6 numbers up

so $9 - 3 = 6$

T	U
7	9
− 4	3
	6

Remember it is **only** possible to take away a smaller number from a larger number.

$7 - 4 = 3$

3̶ ̶7̶ **cannot** be done.

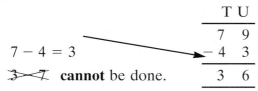

T	U
7	9
− 4	3
3	6

Exercise 3:1

1 Put a cross through any of these subtraction problems that **cannot** be done:

$3 - 5$ $4 - 4$ $7 - 4$ $5 - 6$ $8 - 9$

$2 - 0$ $1 - 8$ $1 - 0$ $3 - 1$ $5 - 6$

Work out the answers.

2   2 4
       − 1 2
      ————

3   5 8
       − 2 3
      ————

4   5 7
       − 1 3
      ————

5   4 8
       − 2 5
      ————

6   4 9 4
       − 2 3 1
      ————

7   3 8 5
       − 1 5 2
      ————

8   5 6 4
       − 2 1 3
      ————

9   2 7 3
       − 1 2 2
      ————

10   4564 − 251

11   573 − 122

12   487 − 244

2   Borrowing

When the digit you are taking away from is not large enough, you have to borrow from another digit.

$$\begin{array}{cc} T & U \\ 8 & 3 \\ -4 & 4 \\ \hline \end{array}$$

3 − 4 cannot be done
We need to borrow from the 8 tens (80).

Write a 1 for the borrowed 10 here.

$$\begin{array}{cc} T & U \\ 8^{7} & {}^{1}3 \\ -4 & 4 \\ \hline \end{array} \longrightarrow \begin{array}{cc} T & U \\ 8^{7} & {}^{1}3 \\ -4 & 4 \\ \hline 3 & 9 \end{array}$$

Now this becomes 13 − 4 = 9

Exercise 3:2

Work out these subtraction sums.

1   6 7
       − 4 8
      ————

2   6 4
       − 3 6
      ————

3   9 4
       − 5 8
      ————

4   7 3
       − 2 7
      ————

5	5 4 − 3 6 ———	**6**	8 4 − 5 8 ———	**7**	6 2 − 4 7 ———	**8**	9 8 − 7 9 ———
9	7 7 − 4 8 ———	**10**	9 2 − 6 7 ———	**11**	8 5 − 4 9 ———	**12**	7 1 − 2 5 ———

13 65 − 38 **14** 94 − 57 **15** 83 − 55

PARENTS AND HELPERS

A number line can sometimes be helpful for counting up or down:

0 1 2 3 4 5 6 7 8 9 10 11 12 13 14 15 16 17 18 19 20

3 Longer problems

You can borrow from any column to the left of the one you are working on.

To do the subtraction 3472 − 1888:

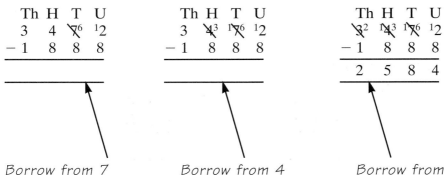

Borrow from 7   Borrow from 4   Borrow from 3

Exercise 3:3

Work out these subtraction sums.

1   5 4 2 7
    –   6 1 8
    ─────────

2   6 5 3 0
    – 2 6 5 2
    ─────────

3   2 1 3 5
    – 1 2 5 0
    ─────────

4   5 3 6 2
    – 1 1 3 3
    ─────────

5   2 3 4 6
    –   5 3 9
    ─────────

6   1 4 2 3
    –   8 7 8
    ─────────

7   1 3 2 0
    –   7 2 1
    ─────────

8   6 2 1 7
    – 5 5 5 5
    ─────────

9   8 2 7 7
    –   5 9 0
    ─────────

10   8 8 8 1
    –   2 3 9
    ─────────

11   2 1 9 3
    –   7 7 7
    ─────────

12   8 4 2 7
    – 4 5 8 0
    ─────────

13   1645 − 756

14   3827 − 1559

15   5748 − 4979

PARENTS AND HELPERS

It is important that each problem is set out correctly, one column under another.
If this presents a problem, then each question could be copied on to squared paper.

4 Borrowing from zero

$4 - 0$ can be done. $0 - 4$ **cannot** be done.

$$\begin{array}{r} 5\ \text{⓪} \\ -\ 1\ \text{⑦} \\ \hline \end{array}$$

Here we have $0 - 7$
It cannot be
done, so

Borrow from
the 5 $\longrightarrow$

$$\begin{array}{r} \cancel{5}^{4}10 \\ -\ 1\ 7 \\ \hline 3\ 3 \end{array}$$

EXAMPLE

$2000 - 304$

Start by borrowing
from the 2.

$$\begin{array}{r} \cancel{2}^{1}\ \cancel{0}^{9}\ \cancel{0}^{9}\ ^{1}0 \\ -\quad 3\ 0\ 4 \\ \hline 1\ 6\ 9\ 6 \end{array}$$

Exercise 3:4

Work out these subtraction sums.

1
$$\begin{array}{r} 2\ 0\ 7 \\ -\quad 4\ 8 \\ \hline \end{array}$$

2
$$\begin{array}{r} 4\ 0\ 5 \\ -\quad 6\ 7 \\ \hline \end{array}$$

3
$$\begin{array}{r} 5\ 0\ 4\ 6 \\ -\quad 1\ 6\ 8 \\ \hline \end{array}$$

4
$$\begin{array}{r} 8\ 0\ 2\ 7 \\ -3\ 3\ 3\ 3 \\ \hline \end{array}$$

5
$$\begin{array}{r} 6\ 2\ 0\ 5 \\ -4\ 8\ 1\ 8 \\ \hline \end{array}$$

6
$$\begin{array}{r} 7\ 0\ 2\ 6 \\ -1\ 2\ 6\ 3 \\ \hline \end{array}$$

7
$$\begin{array}{r} 5\ 0\ 7\ 0 \\ -\quad 4\ 0\ 4 \\ \hline \end{array}$$

8
$$\begin{array}{r} 7\ 0\ 4\ 0 \\ -2\ 5\ 0\ 4 \\ \hline \end{array}$$

9
$$\begin{array}{r} 4\ 0\ 3\ 8 \\ -\quad 3\ 8\ 2 \\ \hline \end{array}$$

10
$$\begin{array}{r} 8\ 0\ 0\ 4 \\ -3\ 7\ 3\ 2 \\ \hline \end{array}$$

11
$$\begin{array}{r} 4\ 0\ 4\ 0 \\ -\quad 3\ 7\ 4 \\ \hline \end{array}$$

12
$$\begin{array}{r} 4\ 0\ 0\ 1 \\ -1\ 2\ 5\ 4 \\ \hline \end{array}$$

13 $3905 - 2446$

14 $7040 - 555$

15 $4000 - 2007$

5   Mixed addition and subtraction problems

Sometimes in a problem you have to decide whether to add or take away.
The wording of the question may give you a clue.

These words may suggest addition: add, sum, total, together.

These words may suggest subtraction: take away, less than, more than,
difference.

Exercise 3:5

For each question decide whether it is an addition or subtraction.
Write out a calculation, then work out the answer.

1   Karen needs £6.85 but has saved only £2.50.
How much more does she need?

£ _____

2   Tony has 685 marbles in his collection.
His friend gives him 139 marbles.
How many marbles does he have now?

_____

3   The number of people at a play is 327 on Friday
and 298 on Saturday.
What was the total attendance?

_____

4   Louise has 106 magazines for sale.
Mary has 48 magazines for sale.
How many more magazines has Louise than Mary?

_____

5   There are 2050 passengers on a ferry.
They are either foot passengers or car passengers.
1098 are car passengers.
How many are foot passengers?

_____

6   Sheraz has test marks of 90 and 63.
What is the difference between his two test marks?

_____

7   There were 879 chickens on one farm, and 763 on another farm.
How many chickens were there altogether?

_____

8   Mark has a bag of sugar containing 475 grams, and
another containing 535 grams.
What is the total weight of the two bags?

_____

9   The attendance at two football matches is 11 430 and 12 880.
What is the total attendance at the two matches?

_____

10 Worsley School let 354 balloons go at a fair.
Prestwich School let 297 balloons go.
How many more balloons were let go by Worsley
than by Prestwich school?

_____

1 Darts

In a game of darts you subtract scores from 501 or 301.

Play a game of darts with a friend, and practise taking your scores away from 501.

The winner is the first to get to 0, as long as the last throw is a double.

2 Numbers

A game for two players. Each player starts with a score of 501.

Pick a two-digit number. Neither of the digits must be a zero.
Take your number away from 501.

Take turns to pick a two-digit number and take it from 501, like darts.

The winner is the first to get to 0, as long as the last number picked is an odd number.

4 Times tables

You will need to know the multiplication tables by heart, or be able to work out the facts quickly. The questions in this chapter will help you practise.

1 Multiplication by 2, 5 and 10

Exercise 4:1

Write down the answer only for these questions.

1 $2 \times 3 =$ _____   **2** $5 \times 2 =$ _____   **3** $6 \times 2 =$ _____

4 $3 \times 5 =$ _____   **5** $9 \times 10 =$ _____   **6** $3 \times 10 =$ _____

7 $9 \times 2 =$ _____   **8** $7 \times 10 =$ _____   **9** $6 \times 5 =$ _____

10 $4 \times 2 =$ _____   **11** $5 \times 10 =$ _____   **12** $9 \times 5 =$ _____

13 Work out the total cost of eight 5p stamps. _____ p

14 There are ten chocolate bars in a box.
How many bars are there in two boxes? _____

15 Seven pairs of socks need washing.
How many socks is this? _____

16 What is the total number of players in five 5-a-side football teams? _____

17 There are six eggs in each egg box.
What is the total number of eggs in 10 egg boxes? _____

18 In a table there are 10 rows, each with 10 boxes.
How many boxes are there altogether? _____

PARENTS AND HELPERS

You need to practise times tables regularly.

There is a multiplication table on page 162 for you to use.

There are two ways to practise times tables:

1   Run through each times table in turn, from × 2 to × 10. It is quite acceptable for a student to work out the answers by lots of adding, but they must be quick at doing this! Eventually they will begin to learn the tables themselves.

2   Read out any two numbers for the student to multiply. You can read off the correct answer from the table. This is more difficult, and should follow on from the first method.

Again it is acceptable to get to the answer by adding, but the student has to know something about the tables to do this, since they should not have enough time to run through the entire table to find the answer.

2   Multiplication by 2, 3, 4, 5 and 10

Exercise 4:2

Write down the answer only for each question.

1 $5 \times 2 =$ _____   **2** $8 \times 4 =$ _____   **3** $7 \times 5 =$ _____

4 $8 \times 2 =$ _____   **5** $4 \times 10 =$ _____   **6** $6 \times 3 =$ _____

7 $4 \times 5 =$ _____   **8** $8 \times 3 =$ _____   **9** $6 \times 10 =$ _____

10 $9 \times 4 =$ _____   **11** $5 \times 5 =$ _____   **12** $10 \times 3 =$ _____

13   There are ten milk bottles in a crate.
How many milk bottles are needed to fill two crates?   _____

14   There are seven days in each week.
How many days are there in four weeks?   _____

15   What is the product of 5 and 10?   _____

16 Tennis balls are sold in tubes of 3.
How many tennis balls are there altogether in 7 tubes? _____

17 An octopus has 8 legs.
What is the total number of legs for 5 octopuses? _____

18 A square has four corners.
How many corners are there altogether in four squares? _____

3　Multiplication by numbers up to 10

Exercise 4:3

Write down the answer only for each question.

1 $2 \times 6 =$ _____

2 $4 \times 2 =$ _____

3 $6 \times 7 =$ _____

4 $5 \times 4 =$ _____

5 $8 \times 8 =$ _____

6 $7 \times 5 =$ _____

7 $3 \times 9 =$ _____

8 $8 \times 6 =$ _____

9 $8 \times 3 =$ _____

10 $9 \times 10 =$ _____

11 $7 \times 7 =$ _____

12 $8 \times 9 =$ _____

13 There are six eggs in a box.
What is the total number of eggs in nine boxes? _____

14 Each table in the canteen can seat 6 students.
How many students can sit at four tables? _____

15 A farmer plants apple trees in rows of 7.
There are 9 rows of trees.
How many trees are there in total? _____

16 To play a game, four players need four counters each.
How many counters are needed? _____

17 What is the product of 5 and 7? _____

18 There are 7 days in a week.
How many days are there in eight weeks? _____

4 Division by 2, 3, 4, 5 and 10

You can use times tables to solve division problems.

Exercise 4:4

Write down the answer only for these questions.

1 18 ÷ 2 = _____   **2** 45 ÷ 5 = _____   **3** 24 ÷ 3 = _____

4 70 ÷ 10 = _____   **5** 36 ÷ 4 = _____   **6** 18 ÷ 2 = _____

7 80 ÷ 10 = _____   **8** 28 ÷ 4 = _____   **9** 30 ÷ 5 = _____

10 16 ÷ 2 = _____   **11** 21 ÷ 3 = _____   **12** 50 ÷ 5 = _____

13 What do you get when you divide
24 by 4? _____

14 A bag of 18 sweets is shared equally
between 3 children.
How many sweets does each child receive? _____

15 How many 2s are there in 14? _____

16 Each table has four legs.
How many tables can be made
with 32 table legs? _____

17 What is the greatest number of £10 notes
you could get for £90? _____

18 A piece of cheese of weight 40g is cut into
five pieces of equal weight.
What is the weight of one piece? _____ g

5 Division by numbers up to 10

Exercise 4:5

Write down the answer only for these questions.

1 22 ÷ 2 = _____   **2** 27 ÷ 3 = _____   **3** 36 ÷ 6 = _____

4 56 ÷ 7 = _____   **5** 35 ÷ 5 = _____   **6** 28 ÷ 4 = _____

7 48 ÷ 8 = _____   **8** 63 ÷ 7 = _____   **9** 42 ÷ 6 = _____

10 72 ÷ 9 = _____   **11** 49 ÷ 7 = _____   **12** 81 ÷ 9 = _____

13 What do you get when you divide 8 into 72? _____

14 A rope 32 metres long is cut into 4 equal pieces.
How long is each piece? _____

15 A bag of 54 counters is divided equally between 9 children.
How many counters does each child receive? _____

16 What is the greatest number of £5 notes you can get for £45? _____

17 Eggs are packed in boxes of 6 eggs each.
How many boxes are needed for 24 eggs? _____

18 A pencil costs 8p.
How many pencils can you buy for 64p? _____

Tables bingo

3		30		11		5		19
	31		46		84		52	
8		99		63		23		89

This is a bingo card.
There are 14 numbers on the bingo card.
All 14 numbers are chosen from the numbers 1 to 99.

You can play this game using a real bingo set, or you can easily make your own.

1 Make at least 10 different bingo cards.

2 You will need some other players for the game. Each player needs a bingo card and counters or pieces of card to cover up the numbers as they are called.

3 Pick a number between 1 and 99 to call out. **BUT**, instead of calling out the number, call out a times table calculation which gives you that number.
(For example, for 56 call out 7×8)
Use the multiplication table grid on page 162 to help you.
Remember to make a note of the numbers you have called out.

4 Continue the game until someone has completed their card.
Make sure you check the card from your own list of numbers called.

For each number called you need to allow some time for the players to work out the answer.
You may also wish to give the players some paper to do their working-outs on.

5   Multiplication

1   Multiplication with a carry

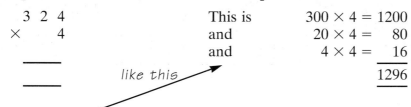

```
  3 2 4        This is     300 × 4 = 1200
×     4        and          20 × 4 =   80
              and            4 × 4 =   16
  _____                              ____
                                     1296
  _____
      like this
```

You can do this
two different ways

like this

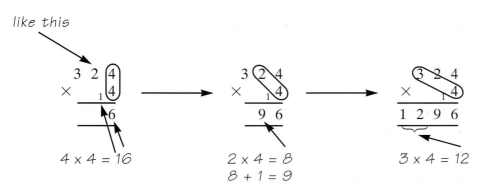

$4 \times 4 = 16$ $2 \times 4 = 8$ $3 \times 4 = 12$
$8 + 1 = 9$

Exercise 5:1

Work out the answers.

1
```
  1 2 3
×     4
_____
_____
```

2
```
  2 0 5
×     5
_____
_____
```

3
```
  1 3 6
×     3
_____
_____
```

4
```
  1 6 1 7
×       2
_____
_____
```

5
```
  8 0 7
×     4
_____
_____
```

6
```
  2 1 0 4
×       6
_____
_____
```

7
```
  4 1 2 8
×       3
_____
_____
```

8
```
  5 0 5
×     5
_____
_____
```

9
```
  2 5 3 8
×       2
_____
_____
```

10
```
  3 0 0 9
×       4
_____
_____
```

11
```
  1 4 1 8
×       5
_____
_____
```

12
```
  2 3 8 1
×       3
_____
_____
```

2   Multiplication with more carries

Exercise 5:2

Work out the answers.

1	6 2 5 × 7	**2**	7 0 6 × 8	**3**	5 7 3 × 4	**4**	6 6 6 × 5
5	6 4 5 × 9	**6**	7 2 8 × 4	**7**	1 6 8 × 6	**8**	1 7 5 × 9
9	1 6 2 4 × 6	**10**	2 5 3 7 × 8	**11**	1 6 2 8 × 9	**12**	1 5 5 4 × 7
13	2 0 9 9 × 4	**14**	3 5 2 8 × 6	**15**	5 3 9 4 × 7	**16**	4 8 7 3 × 9
17	5 4 3 2 × 5	**18**	8 3 7 1 × 8	**19**	2 8 5 7 × 6	**20**	6 4 7 9 × 7

PARENTS AND HELPERS

Any multiplication exercise can be supplemented.
You can write out your own multiplication problems, and check the answers using a calculator.

3   Multiplication by 10, 100, 1000

When multiplying by powers of 10, change the value of each digit:

146×100 so $146 \times 1\!\!\bigcirc\!\!\bigcirc$

Th	H	T	U
	$\times 100$	$\overset{6}{\times 100}$	7
6	7	0	0

move the digits
up two places

$83 \times 10 \quad = 830$
$83 \times 100 \quad = 8300$
$83 \times 1000 = 83000$

For multiples of 10, break the problem down into two stages:

$146 \times 300 = 146 \times 3 \times 100$

$$
\begin{array}{r}
1\ 4\ 6 \\
\times \quad\ \ 3 \\
\hline
5\ 5\ 8
\end{array}
$$ then $558 \times 100 = 55\ 800$

Exercise 5:3

Work out the answers.

1 $274 \times 10 \quad = $ _____   **2** $632 \times 1000 = $ _____

3 $56 \times 100 \quad = $ _____   **4** $60 \times 1000 \quad = $ _____

5 $3109 \times 10 \quad = $ _____   **6** $156 \times 100 \quad = $ _____

7 $113 \times 20 \quad = $ _____   **8** $147 \times 300 \quad = $ _____

9 $215 \times 700 \quad = $ _____   **10** $25 \times 8000 \quad = $ _____

11 $758 \times 40 \quad = $ _____   **12** $35 \times 5000 \quad = $ _____

13 $545 \times 400 \quad = $ _____   **14** $350 \times 90 \quad = $ _____

15 $671 \times 6000 = $ _____   **16** $822 \times 900 \quad = $ _____

4 Multiplying two 2-digit numbers

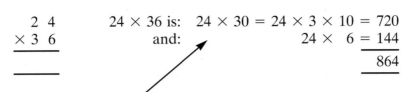

```
  2 4
× 3 6
──────
```

24 × 36 is: 24 × 30 = 24 × 3 × 10 = 720
   and: 24 × 6 = 144
                              ───
                              864

You can do this two different ways

like this

like this

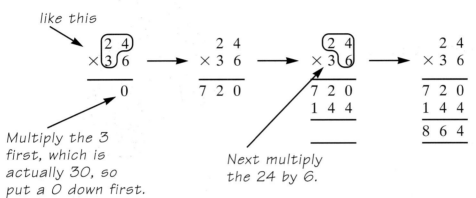

Multiply the 3 first, which is actually 30, so put a 0 down first.

Next multiply the 24 by 6.

Exercise 5:4

Work out the answers

1
```
  3 7
× 1 2
```

2
```
  5 2
× 3 4
```

3
```
  3 6
× 4 1
```

4
```
  2 4
× 2 5
```

5
```
  9 2
× 2 3
```

6
```
  1 3
× 5 9
```

7
```
  2 2
× 3 6
```

8
```
  2 8
× 6 4
```

| 9 | 7 6
× 7 8 | 10 | 9 7
× 8 3 | 11 | 2 6
× 4 2 | 12 | 8 4
× 5 7 |

_____

_____

5   Long multiplication

Exercise 5:5

Work out the answers.

| 1 | 4 2 1
×   2 3 | 2 | 2 0 4
×   3 2 | 3 | 1 6 2
×   2 4 | 4 | 4 1 6
×   3 5 |

_____

| 5 | 3 0 9
×   2 7 | 6 | 6 4 3
×   3 8 | 7 | 7 1 8
×   4 1 | 8 | 7 9 1
×   6 2 |

_____

| 9 | 9 3 5
×   2 1 | 10 | 6 7 5
×   3 7 | 11 | 5 6 1
×   8 1 | 12 | 2 9 8
×   4 3 |

_____

| 13 | 6 8 2
 × 3 3 | 14 | 1 7 2 4
 × 9 3 | 15 | 2 7 3 9
 × 6 3 | 16 | 3 6 0 9
 × 7 1 |

_____   _____   _____   _____

_____   _____   _____   _____

PARENTS AND HELPERS

You should always check your answer by using approximation.

For example, 29×12 is about $30 \times 10 \rightarrow 300$

29×12 actually gives 348, so the approximation is very near to the actual answer.

1 Setting up a multiplication table on a spreadsheet

If you have a computer with a spreadsheet program you can use it to make a multiplication table.

Set it up like this:

	A	B	C	D
1		1	2	3
2	1	B1*B2	C1*C2	D1*D2
3	2	B1*B3	C1*C3	D1*D3
4	3	B1*B4	C1*C4	D1*D4

Extend this table downwards for as far as you wish to go.
You can then print out a complete multiplication table.

If you want to make a table for bigger values, just change the values in the first row of the table.
For the 20 times table:

	A	B	C	D
1	1	21	22	23
2	2			
	3			

2 Unit times

Look at these multiplication sums.

$$13 \times 22 = 28\mathbf{6}$$
$$42 \times 63 = 264\mathbf{6}$$
$$123 \times 62 = 762\mathbf{6}$$
$$82 \times 113 = 926\mathbf{6}$$

The units in all the answers are 6. We could call 6 the **units answer** in all these problems.

Now look at the units of the two numbers that have been multiplied:

eg $1\mathbf{3} \times 2\mathbf{2} = 28\mathbf{6}$

Can you explain what is happening to all the units numbers in the multiplication sums above?

Work out the units answer to these problems.
Write them in the table.

Problem	Units answer
72×43	
93×112	
12×63	
730×49	

Write down more multiplication problems that give you units answers of 6:

Problem	Units answer
	6
	6
	6
	6

Find five multiplication problems that give units answers:
0, 1, 2, 3, 4, 5, 6, 7, 8, 9

Check your answers using a calculator.

6 Division

1 Division with remainders

When numbers do not divide exactly we are left with remainders.

$$
\begin{array}{r}
6 \\
7 \overline{)4\ 5^3 3\ 8}
\end{array}
\longrightarrow
\begin{array}{r}
6\ 4 \\
7 \overline{)4\ 5^3 3^5 8}
\end{array}
$$

6 × 7 = 42   **4** × 7 = 28
3 remainder   **5** remainder

$$
\begin{array}{r}
6\ 4\ 8\ \text{r2} \\
7 \overline{)4\ 5^3 3^5 8}
\end{array}
$$

8 × 7 = 56
2 remainder   So 4538 ÷ 7 = 648 r2

1 × 7 = 7
2 × 7 = 14
3 × 7 = 21
4 × 7 = 28
5 × 7 = 35
6 × 7 = 42
7 × 7 = 49
8 × 7 = 56
9 × 7 = 63
10 × 7 = 70

Exercise 6:1

Work out the answers, showing any remainders.

1   4)1 8 2

2   6)7 9 9

3   7)9 6 8

4   3)8 0 0 5

5   8)9 8 7

6   6)2 7 2

7   9)7 9 0

8   3)8 9 0 3

9   7)8 6 8 5

10   8)9 0 4 5

11   4)2 9 7 4

12   6)2 8 1 0

PARENTS AND HELPERS

You cannot check these answers with a calculator, as calculators do not know how to work out remainders! They give them as decimal answers, but the decimal part is **not** the remainder.

If the students work out the times table used in every question it will help them to remember their times tables.

2 Division with decimal answers

Remainders can be written in the form of a decimal.

$$\overset{\textcircled{6}}{8\,)\overline{5\,1^31\,4}} \longrightarrow \overset{6\textcircled{4}}{8\,)\overline{5\,1^33^14}}$$

6 × 8 = 48
   3 remainder

4 × 8 = 32
   1 remainder

$$\overset{6\,4\,1}{8\,)\overline{5\,1^33^14^6}}$$

$$\overset{6\,4\,1}{8\,)\overline{5\,1^33^14.^60}}$$

1 × 8 = 8
   6 remainder

Add .0 so you can
carry on dividing.

$$\overset{6\,4\,1.\,7\,5}{8\,)\overline{5\,1^33^14.^60^40}}$$

So 5134 ÷ 8 = 641.75

1 × 8 =	8
2 × 8 =	16
3 × 8 =	24
4 × 8 =	32
5 × 8 =	40
6 × 8 =	48
7 × 8 =	56
8 × 8 =	64
9 × 8 =	72
10 × 8 =	80

Exercise 6:2

Work out the answers, showing any remainders as decimals.

1 $4\,)\overline{4\,9}$

2 $6\,)\overline{6\,2\,7}$

3 $2\,)\overline{7\,9\,5}$

4 $8\,)\overline{1\,2\,1}$

5 $2\,)\overline{1\,5\,6\,9}$

6 $4\,)\overline{1\,7\,4\,3}$

7 $8\,)\overline{1\,8\,1}$

8 $6\,)\overline{2\,6\,6\,1}$

9 $2\,)\overline{2\,7\,8\,9}$

10 $6\,)\overline{2\,2\,5\,9}$

11 $8\,)\overline{1\,0\,1\,9}$

12 $4\,)\overline{1\,6\,6\,3}$

PARENTS AND HELPERS

You **can** check these with a calculator, because calculators give their remainders in decimal form.

3   Division by 10, 100, 1000

To divide by powers of 10, change the value of each digit.

$1460 \div 100$

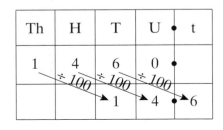

(0) ← ———— *Not needed*

For multiples of 10, break the problem down into two or more steps:

$$140 \div 200 = 146 \div 2 \div 100$$
$$= 73 \div 100 = 0.73$$

Exercise 6:3

Work out the answers.

1 $30 \div 10 =$ _____

2 $5000 \div 1000 =$ _____

3 $200 \div 100 =$ _____

4 $70\,000 \div 1000 =$ _____

5 $8000 \div 100 =$ _____

6 $9000 \div 100 =$ _____

7 $400 \div 100 =$ _____

8 $6000 \div 2000 =$ _____

9 $1800 \div 60 =$ _____

10 $36\,000 \div 900 =$ _____

11 $1500 \div 300 =$ _____

12 $24\,000 \div 8000 =$ _____

13 $20\,000 \div 400 =$ _____

14 $350\,000 \div 70 =$ _____

15 $160\,000 \div 8000 =$ _____

16 $100\,000 \div 500 =$ _____

4 Long division

EXAMPLE

8688 ÷ 16
Break the problem down into stages.

$1 \times 16 = 16$
$2 \times 16 = 32$
$3 \times 16 = 48$
$4 \times 16 = 64$
$5 \times 16 = 80$
$6 \times 16 = 96$
$7 \times 16 = 112$
$8 \times 16 = 128$
$9 \times 16 = 144$
$10 \times 16 = 160$

16)8 6 8 8   ⑤

5 × 16 = 80
remainder
is **6**

16)8 6⁶8 8   5 ④

4 × 16 = 64
remainder
is **4**

16)8 6⁶8⁴8   5 4 3

3 × 16 = 48
no remainder

So 8688 ÷ 16 = 543

Exercise 6:4

Work out the answers.

1 12)1 5 8 4 0

2 21)3 0 4 5

3 26)6 2 6 6

4 14)3 2 6 2

5 15)5 1 3 0

6 32)1 2 9 2 8

7 13)6 0 4 5

8 45)3 5 2 3 5

9 31)2 7 0 9 4

10 38)2 6 9 0 4

11 52)1 8 3 0 4

12 47)4 2 1 5 9

5 Remainders with words

Read each problem and fill in the answers.

1 A lift can carry a maximum of 8 people.
How many trips of the lift are needed for 50 people?

_____

2 It takes Darren 20 minutes to service a vacuum cleaner.
How many vacuum cleaners can he service in 3½ hours?

_____

3 How many 20-litre containers can be filled completely from
a tank containing 98 litres of water?

_____

4 Billy has £3 pocket money each week.
How many weeks will it take him to save £25?

_____

5 100 pence is to be shared equally between 6 children.
How many pence does each child receive?

_____

6 Tiles are bought in boxes of 10. Julie needs 82 tiles.
How many boxes will she need to buy?

_____

7 A box can hold 6 eggs.
How many boxes can be filled completely from a basket of 70 eggs?

_____

8 Powder is bought in 7 kg drums. 50 kg of powder is needed.
How many drums are needed?

FINEST
QUALITY
POWDER

7kg

_____

9 A taxi can carry 4 people.
How many taxis are needed for 50 people?

_____

10 A tube contains 8 sweets.
How many tubes can be filled completely from a bag of 100 sweets?

_____

6 Multiplication and division problems

You will need to decide which method to use to solve the problem.
Show your working carefully.

1   There are five lessons per day in a school timetable.
How many lessons are there in 9 days?

2   A television stand has 4 legs.
How many television stands could be made from
36 legs?

3   What is the product of 87 and 9?

4   A train carriage can seat 142 passengers. A train has 8 full carriages.
How many passengers are on the train?

5   Jimmy can fit 6 large boxes in his van.
How many trips does he make to move 48 large boxes?

6   A cassette player costs £23.
What is the total cost of 421 cassette players?

7   Prize money of £4878 is shared equally between 9 people.
How much does each person receive?

8   13 662 g of powder is packed into 22 containers.
What weight of powder is in each container?

9   A packet can hold 15 marbles.
How many packets are needed for 14 205 marbles?

10   A large box contains 12 eggs.
What is the total number of eggs in 327 large boxes?

Divisions of 100

You will need a calculator.

a   Find all the even numbers between 2 and 98 that
     divide into 100 exactly (without any remainders
     or decimal answers).

b   Make a list of all the even numbers less than 20.
     Use a calculator to divide these numbers into 100.
     Write down the full answers given by your calculator.
     Do these numbers make a pattern?

     Try this with even numbers larger than 20.

c   Find all the odd numbers between 1 and 99 that divide into 100 exactly
     (without any remainders or decimal answers).

d   Make a list of all the odd numbers less than 20.
     Use a calculator to divide these numbers into 100.
     Write down the full answers given by your calculator.
     Can you see a pattern in the decimal numbers?

     Try this with odd numbers larger than 20.

e   What type of numbers as dividers will give you a decimal answer that
     goes on and on?

7 Decimals

1 Decimals and fractions

DECIMAL	H 100	T 10	U 1	•	t $\frac{1}{10}$	h $\frac{1}{100}$	th $\frac{1}{1000}$	FRACTION
0.057			0	•	0	5	7	$\frac{57}{1000}$
14.42		1	4	•	4	2		$14\frac{42}{100}$

The value of the last digit tells you how small the fraction is.

FRACTION	H 100	T 10	U 1	•	t $\frac{1}{10}$	h $\frac{1}{100}$	th $\frac{1}{1000}$	DECIMAL
$\frac{3}{1000}$			0	•	0	0	3	0.003
$1\frac{7}{100}$			1	•	0	7		1.07

You have to put in these zeros.

Exercise 7:1

Complete these tables.

DECIMAL	H	T	U	•	t	h	th	FRACTION
0.7				•				
0.67				•				
0.08				•				
2.37				•				
1.004				•				

FRACTION	H	T	U	•	t	h	th	DECIMAL
$\frac{3}{100}$				•				
$2\frac{7}{10}$				•				
$\frac{11}{1000}$				•				
$4\frac{3}{100}$				•				
$3\frac{9}{10}$				•				

2 Using decimals in estimation

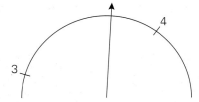

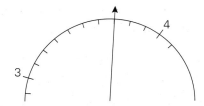

Divide the scale into parts to help you estimate the reading.

Each part is 0.1 So the arrow is pointing at 3.7

Exercise 7:2

Estimate the readings on each scale or dial.

1

| 6cm | | 7cm |

_____cm

2

3
2
amps
4

_____ amps

3

0
3   1
kg
2

_____ kg

4

0
1
g

_____ g

5

7
6
5
mm

_____mm

6

3   4   5

_____

7

7 | 8
m

_____ m

8

40
30   50
20   mph   60

_____ mph

9

3
2
1
°C   0

10

5   6   7
litres

_____ litres   _____ °C

3 Ordering decimals

To write decimal numbers in order, first look at the figures at the front of the decimal (the most significant figures).

Write in descending order (largest first):   0.745   0.607   0.753   0.643   0.642

Order by:

first digits $(\frac{1}{10})$	second digits $(\frac{1}{100})$	third digits $(\frac{1}{1000})$
0.745	0.753	0.753
0.753	0.745	0.745
0.607	0.642	0.643
0.643	0.643	0.642
0.652	0.607	0.607

Descending order: 0.753   0.745   0.643   0.642   0.607

In ascending order this would be: 0.607   0.642   0.643   0.745   0.753

Exercise 7:3

Write these decimals in descending order:

1 0.022, 2.0, 2.02, 0.220

2 0.8, 0.08, 0.008, 8.0

3 1.2, 2.1, 0.12, 0.21

4 0.556, 0.572, 0.574, 0.565

5 9.904, 9.99, 9.804, 9.9

6 7.202, 7.305, 7.306, 7.204

Write these decimals in ascending order:

7 8.701, 8.88, 8.801, 8.8

8 1.25, 0.125, 0.525, 0.55

_____

_____

9 4.222, 4.022, 4.202

10 1.08, 9.8, 10.8, 9.08

_____

_____

11 0.0266, 0.0206, 0.06606

12 3.33, 3.033, 3.303

_____

_____

4 Adding decimals

To add decimals write them in an addition sum.

The figures with the same place value should be under each other.
The decimal points should line up under each other.

EXAMPLE

$2.05 + 4 + 0.7 + 12.564$

4 units
is the same as 4.0

$$
\begin{array}{r}
2.05 \\
4 \\
0.7 \\
12.564 \\
\hline
19.314 \\
\hline
\end{array}
$$

Exercise 7:4

Write each problem as an addition sum, and work out the answer.

1 $3.67 + 4 + 0.09$

2 $3.78 + 0.79 + 8.5$

_____

_____

3   4.58 + 0.09 + 5.8

———————

4   0.86 + 9.5 + 0.07

———————

5   7.3 + 0.06 + 8 + 0.75

———————

6   2.376 + 7 + 12.75 + 0.875

———————

7   0.69 + 3 + 2.82 + 0.095

———————

8   12.75 + 0.9 + 8.67

———————

9   2.06 + 3.5 + 4.44

———————

10   0.607 + 0.089 + 2.5

———————

11   0.836 + 0.7 + 4 + 6.47

———————

12   5.3 + 0.075 + 0.85 + 8

———————

PARENTS AND HELPERS

Calculators can be used to check the answers to these problems.
These questions should all be attempted first without a calculator.

5 Subtracting decimals

To take away decimals, write them in a subtraction sum.

The digits with the same place value should be under each other.
The decimal points should line up.
Fill in gaps in the numbers with zeros, particularly in the numbers you are taking away from.

$$4.32 - 1.404$$

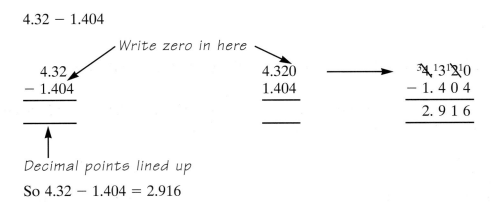

Write zero in here

$$
\begin{array}{r}
4.32 \\
-\,1.404 \\
\hline
\end{array}
\qquad
\begin{array}{r}
4.320 \\
1.404 \\
\hline
\end{array}
\qquad\longrightarrow\qquad
\begin{array}{r}
^3\!4.^{13}1^{12}2^{1}0 \\
-\,1.4\;0\;4 \\
\hline
2.9\;1\;6
\end{array}
$$

Decimal points lined up

So $4.32 - 1.404 = 2.916$

Exercise 7:5

Write each problem as a subtraction sum and work out the answers.

1 $6.574 - 2.481$

2 $4 - 0.38$

3 $4.664 - 3.687$

4 $5.044 - 2.945$

5 $7.3 - 6.91$

6 $6.071 - 5.094$

7 $9.08 - 8.99$

8 $1.2 - 1.089$

9 $0.41 - 0.093$ **10** $0.606 - 0.57$

_____   _____

11 $0.13 - 0.012$ **12** $4.03 - 3.092$

_____   _____

6   Multiplication with one decimal number

When multiplying a decimal number we have to make sure the answer is given to the same accuracy as the number we start with.

6.4×7

One number after the decimal point.

$$
\begin{array}{r}
6\,4 \\
\times\ _2 7 \\
\hline
4\,4\,8
\end{array}
$$

$6.4 \times 7 = 44.8$

Write the answer with one number after the decimal point.

2.65×18

Two numbers after the decimal point.

$$
\begin{array}{r}
2\,6\,5 \\
\times\ \ 1\,8 \\
\hline
2\,6\,5\,0 \\
2\ 1^5 2\,0 \\
\hline
4\,7\,7\,0
\end{array}
$$

$2.65 \times 18 = 47.70$

Write the answer with two numbers after the decimal point.

Exercise 7:6

Write each problem as a multiplication sum and work out the answers.

1 7.8×9 **2** 6.55×9

_____   _____

3 6.135×8 **4** 2.13×8

_____   _____

5 3.026×4

_____

6 7.06×8

_____

7 14.6×17

_____

8 2.45×16

_____

9 1.55×23

_____

10 1.58×24

_____

11 2.15×31

_____

12 2.86×34

_____

7   Multiplication with two decimal numbers

When multiplying two decimal numbers together, we need to make sure the answer is given to the same accuracy as the numbers we start with.

$$2.\underline{06} \times 0.\underline{4}$$

Altogether there are three numbers after the decimal point.

$$
\begin{array}{r}
2\,0\,6 \\
\times \;\;\, {}_2 4 \\
\hline
8\,2\,4 \\
\end{array}
$$

$$0.824$$

Write the answer with three numbers after the decimal point.

$$4.\underline{69} \times 1.\underline{2}$$

Altogether there are three numbers after the decimal point.

$$
\begin{array}{r}
4\,6\,9 \\
\times \;\;\; 1\,2 \\
\hline
4\,6\,9\,0 \\
{}_{1\,1}9^1 3^1 8 \\
\hline
5\,6\,2\,8 \\
\end{array}
$$

$$5.628$$

Write the answer with three numbers after the decimal point.

Exercise 7:7

Write each problem as a multiplication problem and work out the answer.

1 1.3×0.2

_____

2 31.2×0.4

_____

3 4.2×0.7

_____

4 46.9×0.5

_____

5 3.6×0.3

_____

6 1.6×0.4

_____

7 7.06×11

_____

8 1.05×2.1

_____

9 42.5×1.3

_____

10 1.36×0.22

_____

11 21.8×3.1

_____

12 39.4×0.42

_____

8 Multiplication and division by 10 and 100

When multiplying by 10, 100 or multiples of these, the effect is to move the digits to the left. You may need to add zeros when the figures are moved.

3.15×10

H	T	U •	$\frac{1}{10}$	$\frac{1}{100}$
		3	1 •	2

$3.15 \times 10 = 31.5$

When dividing by 10, 100 or multiples of these, the effect is to move the digits to the right. You may need to add zeros when the figures are moved.

$2.4 \div 100$

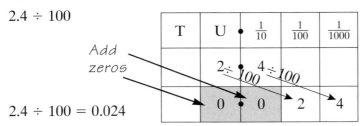

$2.4 \div 100 = 0.024$

Exercise 7:8

Write down the answers to these problems.

1 2.54×10 **2** 1.042×100 **3** $0.13 \div 10$

_____   _____   _____

4 $1.75 \div 100$ **5** 0.055×100 **6** $1.042 \div 10$

_____   _____   _____

7 7.05×10 **8** 0.51×10 **9** 0.6×100

_____   _____   _____

10 $5.4 \div 10$ **11** $1.2 \div 100$ **12** 9.914×100

_____   _____   _____

PARENTS AND HELPERS

The decimals in this exercise can be drawn in a grid as in the examples for 3.15 and 2.4 above, if this helps in completing these problems.

9 Dividing decimals

When dividing into a decimal, keep the decimal points lined up.
You should not leave any remainders, but should work out your answers as decimals.

$11.3 \div 8$

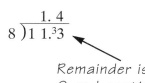

$$\begin{array}{r} 1.\,4 \\ 8\,\overline{)1\,1.^33} \end{array} \qquad \begin{array}{r} 1.\,4\,1\,2\,5 \\ 8\,\overline{)1\,1.^33^10^20^40} \end{array}$$

*Remainder is 1, so add
0 and continue dividing.*

Exercise 7:9

Work out the answers:

1

$3\,\overline{)4\,0.\,2\,6}$

2

$7\,\overline{)1\,7.\,0\,1}$

3

$5\,\overline{)7\,2.\,5\,5}$

4

$6\,\overline{)1\,2.\,8\,6\,1}$

5

$4\,\overline{)0.\,6\,2\,9\,2}$

6

$8\,\overline{)1\,8\,9.\,0}$

7

$3\,\overline{)1\,4\,2.\,0\,2}$

8

$5\,\overline{)2\,8.\,0\,3\,6}$

9

$4\,\overline{)4.\,1\,7\,4}$

10

$6\,\overline{)1\,5\,9.\,0\,8\,4}$

11

$8\,\overline{)7\,5.\,8\,0\,4}$

12

$7\,\overline{)3\,4\,3.\,2\,8}$

Number parts

Any number can be split into parts.
What do you get when you multiply these parts together?

Section A: splitting into 2 parts

For the number 5:

Parts of 5 are: 5 and 0
              4 and 1
              3 and 2
              1.5 and 3.5
              2.5 and 2.5

Multiply the parts together in their pairs:
              $5 \times 0 = 0$
              $4 \times 1 = 4$
              $3 \times 2 = 6$
              $1.5 \times 3.5 = 5.25$
              $2.5 \times 2.5 = 6.25$

The maximum you can get is $2.5 \times 2.5 = 6.25$

Now try some numbers yourself: 6, 7, 8, 9, 10, etc.

Split each number into 2 parts. Multiply these parts together.
Find the 2 parts that will give you the maximum answer.

Can you find an easy rule to help you find the maximum for any number?

Section B: splitting into 3 parts

EXAMPLE

For the number 5:

Parts of 5 are: 1, 1 and 3
1, 2 and 2
1.5, 1.5 and 2

Multiply them:
$1 \times 1 \times 3 = 3$
$1 \times 2 \times 2 = 4$
$1.5 \times 1.5 \times 2 = 4.5$

Try them all and find the maximum answer.

Now try some numbers yourself: 6, 7, 8, 9, 10, etc.

Split each number into 3 parts. Multiply these parts together.
Find the 3 parts that will give you the maximum answer.
Can you find an easy rule to help you find the maximum for any number?

Section C: splitting into 4 parts

Do this in the same way as 2 and 3 parts above.
As before, start with 5:
$1, 1, 1, 2; \quad 1 \times 1 \times 1 \times 2 = 2$

Work through this task in the same way as for 3 parts.

8 Number properties and sequences

1 Number names

An **even number** is in the 2 times table.
An **odd number** *is not* in the 2 times table.
A **multiple** is in the times table of a number.
A **factor** is a number that goes into another number.

Exercise 8:1

| 2 | 3 | 8 | 9 | 13 | 15 | 20 |

From this list of numbers write down:

1 all the odd numbers _____

2 all the even numbers _____

3 all the multiples of 5 _____

4 all the multiples of 3 _____

5 all the numbers that are factors of 12 _____

| 3 | 5 | 6 | 12 | 25 | 30 | 40 |

From this list of numbers write down:

6 all the odd numbers _____

7 all the even numbers _____

8 all the multiples of 5 _____

9 all the multiples of 4 _____

10 all the numbers that are factors of 15 _____

Write down all the factors of each number:

11 42: _____

12 16: _____

13 20: _____

14 15: _____

15 21: _____

16 24: _____

PARENTS AND HELPERS

We use multiples of numbers a lot in this chapter. A good knowledge of times tables will help.

This is a good time for pupils to revise the work they may have already done by learning their times tables. They should know them by this stage.

---

2 Common multiples and factors

Multiples of 4: 4, 8, 12, 16, 20, 24, 28, 32, 36, 40

Multiples of 5: 5, 10, 15, 20, 25, 30, 35, 40

Two **common multiples** of 4 and 5 are the numbers 20 and 40.
The **lowest common multiple** of 4 and 5 is 20.

Factors of 16: 1, 2, 4, 8, 16
Factors of 24: 1, 2, 3, 4, 6, 8, 12, 24

The **common factors** of 16 and 24 are 2, 4 and 8.
The **highest common factor** of 16 and 24 is 8.

Exercise 8:2

Find the first three common multiples of each pair:

1 2 and 3: _____

2 4 and 6: _____

3 3 and 4: _____

4 2 and 5: _____

Find the lowest common multiple of each pair:

5 10 and 15: _____ **6** 2 and 3: _____

7 4 and 12: _____ **8** 6 and 9: _____

Find the common factors of each pair:

9 18 and 24: _____ **10** 9 and 21: _____

11 40 and 60: _____ **12** 14 and 35: _____

Find the highest common factor of each pair:

13 36 and 45: _____ **14** 32 and 48: _____

15 20 and 30: _____ **16** 35 and 63: _____

3 Special numbers

Prime number: a number that has no factors other than 1 and itself.

Prime factor: a factor of a number that is also a prime number.

Square numbers: numbers that make the series 1, 4, 9, 16, 25, using 1×1, 2×2, 3×3, etc.

Triangle numbers: numbers that make the series 1, 3, 6, 10, 15, etc.

Exercise 8:3

1 Write down the first 10 prime numbers:

_____

2 Write down the first 10 square numbers:

_____

3 Write down the first 10 triangle numbers:

_____

4 Circle any prime numbers in these lists:

2   6   10   13   15   18   1   4   5   8   11   14   21

5   9   12   15   19   21   25   20   23   25   29   39   41

5 Circle any square numbers in these lists:

3   4   21   30   44   64   16   20   33   49   53   88   100

9   10   22   36   40   48   25   30   44   64   70   81   95

6 Write down the prime factors of these numbers:

a 36: _____   **b** 72: _____

c 96: _____   **d** 120: _____

7 Work out:

a 5^2: _____   **b** 8^2: _____

c the square of 6: _____   **d** the square of 1: _____

4 Sequence of diagrams

Diagram 1   Diagram 2   Diagram 3

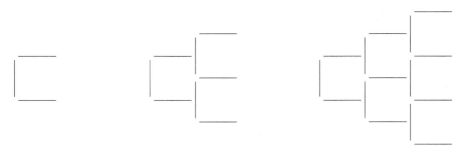

Diagram number	1	2	3	4	5
Number of sticks	3	8	15		

+5 +7 +9 24 +11 35

You can work out the number differences.

Check by drawing the next diagram:

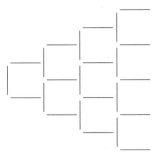

Diagram 4

Exercise 8:4

Complete the table for each sequence.

1

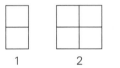

Diagram	1	2	3	4	5
Number of squares	2	4	6		

2

Diagram	1	2	3	4	5
Number of sticks	3	6	9		

3

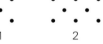

Diagram	1	2	3	4	5
Number of dots	5	8	11		

4

Diagram	1	2	3	4	5
Number of sticks	4	7	10		

5

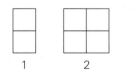

Diagram	1	2	3	4	5
Distance around perimeter	6	8	10		

6

Diagram	1	2	3	4	5
Number of sticks	3	5	7		

5 Number sequences

To continue a number sequence, or find missing terms, first find the differences between the numbers.

Find the missing terms in these number sequences.

4, 6, 8, 10, _____ , _____   15, 23, 31, _____ , _____ , 55

First find the differences:

4,   6,   8,   10, _____ , _____   15, 23, 31, _____ , _____
+ 2 + 2 + 2   + 8 + 8

Continue adding 2:   Continue adding 8:

The correct last term.

4, 6, 8, 10, 12, 14   15, 23, 31, 39, 47, 55
+ 2+ 2   + 8 + 8 + 8

Exercise 8:5

Find the missing terms in the number sequences.

1 20, 31, 42, _____ , _____   **2** 31, 27, 23, 19, _____ , _____

3 3, 5, 8, _____ , _____ , 23   **4** 10, 13, 18, _____ , _____ , 45

5 15, 16, 21, 30, _____ , _____   **6** 9, _____ , _____ , 24, 29, 34

7 17, 23, 29, 35, _____ , _____   **8** 17, 20, 23, 26, _____ , _____

9 16, 25, 34, _____ , _____ , 61   **10** 9, 16, 23, 30, _____ , _____

11 _____ , _____ , 14, 11, 8, 5   **12** 17, _____ , _____ , 26, 29, 32

PARENTS AND HELPERS

Investigating and creating number sequences can be fun!

Pupils can make up their own sequences:

First decide what you want to add on each time:

$+ 1, + 2, + 3, + 4$

Then choose the starting point:

2 ⤷ 3 ⤷ 5 ⤷ 8 . . .

  $+ 1$ $+ 2$ $+ 3$

Write down the first 20 terms.

Give the number sequence to someone else, and ask them to find the rule.

Here are some other ideas you can use to make up your own number sequences:

$+ 1, - 2, + 3, - 4, + 5, \ldots$

$+ 3, + 3, + 3, + 3, + 3, \ldots$

$- 2, - 3, - 4, - 5, - 6, \ldots$

6 Finding rules

All number sequences have a rule:

Term number	1	2	3	4	5	6
Term	1	4	7	10		

The term numbers have a connection with the terms:

1	$\rightarrow$	1
2	$\rightarrow$	4
3	$\rightarrow$	7
4	$\rightarrow$	10

The number differences are + 3. Does this help you get to the rule?

The connection is the rule $\times 3 - 2$.

The table can be completed using the rule:

Term number	1	2	3	4	5	6
Term	1	4	7	10	13	16

Exercise 8:6

In each question find the rule of the number sequence, and complete the table.

1

Term number	1	2	3	4	5	6
Term	3	5	7	9		

Rule _____

2

Term number	1	2	3	4	5	6
Term	5	7	9	11		

Rule _____

3

Term number	1	2	3	4	5	6
Term	5	8	11	14		

Rule _____

4

Term number	1	2	3	4	5	6
Term	5	9	13	17		

Rule _____

5

Term number	1	2	3	4	5	6
Term	1	3	5	7		

Rule _____

6

Term number	1	2	3	4	5	6
Term	1	4	7	10		

Rule _____

7

Term number	1	2	3	4	5	6
Term	3	7	11	15		

Rule _____

8

Term number	1	2	3	4	5	6
Term	7	12	17	22		

Rule _____

1   Prime number display

You can make a display to show all the prime numbers less than 100.

This is a **hundred square:**

1	2	3	4	5	6	7	8	9	10
11	12	13	14	15	16	17	18	19	20
21	22	23	24	25	26	27	28	29	30
31	32	33	34	35	36	37	38	39	40
41	42	43	44	45	46	47	48	49	50
51	52	53	54	55	56	57	58	59	60
61	62	63	64	65	66	67	68	69	70
71	72	73	74	75	76	77	78	79	80
81	82	83	84	85	86	87	88	89	90
91	92	93	94	95	96	97	98	99	100

a Colour in the multiples of 2 (in the 2 times table).

b Colour in the multiples of 3 (in the 3 times table).

c Colour in the multiples of 4 (in the 4 times table).

d Carry on colouring in the multiples of all the numbers from 1 to 99. You may wish to use different colours for each set of multiples.

The numbers left uncoloured at the end are the prime numbers.

2   Dots and lines

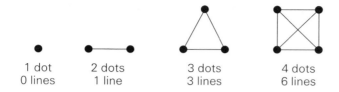

1 dot	2 dots	3 dots	4 dots
0 lines	1 line	3 lines	6 lines

In the diagrams, each dot is connected to every other dot by a line.

Draw the diagrams for 5 dots and 6 dots.

Complete the table to show the information for all your diagrams.

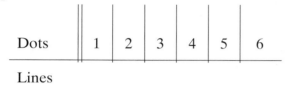

Dots	1	2	3	4	5	6
Lines						

Find out how many lines are needed for these numbers of dots:

a 10 dots:

b 15 dots:

c 20 dots:

Find a way to work out (easily) how many lines you need for much larger diagrams, such as 20 dots or 30 dots.

9 Fractions – addition and subtraction

1 Simple fractions

There are 4 squares.
3 are shaded.
The fraction of the whole shape that is shaded is 3 squares out of 4.

We write this as a fraction as $\frac{3}{4}$

Exercise 9:1

Write down the fraction of the diagram that is shaded.

1

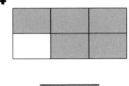

_____

2

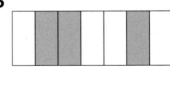

_____

3

_____

4

_____

5

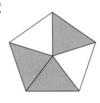

6

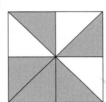

_____

Shade the diagram to show the fractions asked for.

7

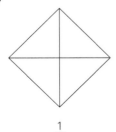

$\frac{1}{4}$

8

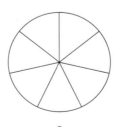

$\frac{3}{7}$

9

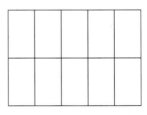

$\frac{7}{10}$

10

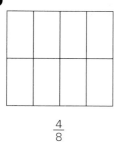

$$\frac{4}{8}$$

11

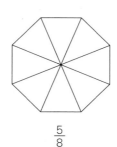

$$\frac{5}{8}$$

12

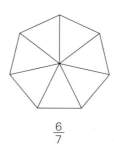

$$\frac{6}{7}$$

2 Equivalent fractions

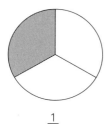

$$\frac{1}{3}$$

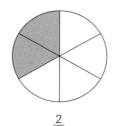

$$\frac{2}{6}$$

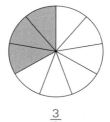

$$\frac{3}{9}$$

These shaded sections are all the same.

They show the **equivalent** fractions $\dfrac{1}{3} = \dfrac{2}{6} = \dfrac{3}{9}$

When two fractions are equivalent, one is a **multiple** of the other.

$$\frac{2}{3} = \frac{}{12} \qquad\qquad \frac{}{7} = \frac{20}{35}$$

$$\frac{2}{3} = \frac{}{12} \qquad\qquad \frac{}{7} = \frac{20}{35}$$

$\times 4$ $\qquad\qquad\qquad$ $\times 5$

The second fraction is 4 times as large as the first.

The second fraction is 5 times as large as the first.

$\times 4$ $\qquad\qquad\qquad\qquad$ $\times 5$

So $\qquad \dfrac{2}{3} = \dfrac{8}{12} \qquad\qquad \dfrac{4}{7} = \dfrac{20}{35}$

$\times 4$ $\qquad\qquad\qquad\qquad$ $\times 5$

Exercise 9:2

Fill in the missing numbers.

1 $\dfrac{2}{3} = \dfrac{}{6} = \dfrac{}{9} = \dfrac{8}{}$
        2 $\dfrac{4}{6} = \dfrac{}{12} = \dfrac{12}{} = \dfrac{}{24}$

3 $\dfrac{3}{5} = \dfrac{6}{} = \dfrac{}{15} = \dfrac{}{20}$
        4 $\dfrac{3}{4} = \dfrac{}{8} = \dfrac{9}{} = \dfrac{}{16}$

5 $\dfrac{3}{4} = \dfrac{}{12}$
   6 $\dfrac{1}{3} = \dfrac{}{15}$
   7 $\dfrac{2}{3} = \dfrac{}{9}$
   8 $\dfrac{3}{4} = \dfrac{}{20}$

9 $\dfrac{4}{5} = \dfrac{}{10}$
   10 $\dfrac{4}{5} = \dfrac{}{15}$
   11 $\dfrac{5}{6} = \dfrac{35}{}$
   12 $\dfrac{2}{3} = \dfrac{8}{}$

3 Ordering fractions

To write fractions in ascending or descending order, we first need to write them with the same common denominator.

Write in descending order (largest first): $\dfrac{3}{4}, \dfrac{5}{6}, \dfrac{8}{12}$

The common denominator of 4, 6 and 12 is 12.
We need to change all the denominators to 12:

$$\overset{\times\,3}{\dfrac{3}{4}} = \underset{\times\,3}{\dfrac{9}{12}} \qquad \overset{\times\,2}{\dfrac{5}{6}} = \underset{\times\,2}{\dfrac{10}{12}} \qquad \dfrac{8}{12} \quad \textit{No change}$$

In descending order: $\dfrac{10}{12}, \dfrac{9}{12}, \dfrac{8}{12}$

The original fractions in descending order: $\dfrac{5}{6}, \dfrac{3}{4}, \dfrac{8}{12}$

Ascending order is: $\dfrac{8}{12}, \dfrac{3}{4}, \dfrac{5}{6}$

Exercise 9:3

Find the common denominators and then write these fractions in descending order.

1 $\dfrac{2}{3}$, $\dfrac{4}{5}$

2 $\dfrac{3}{8}$, $\dfrac{2}{5}$

3 $\dfrac{2}{7}$, $\dfrac{4}{9}$

_____

_____

_____

4 $\dfrac{3}{10}$, $\dfrac{2}{7}$

5 $\dfrac{3}{6}$, $\dfrac{7}{8}$

6 $\dfrac{2}{3}$, $\dfrac{3}{5}$

_____

_____

_____

Use common denominators to write these fractions in ascending order.

7 $\dfrac{5}{8}$, $\dfrac{2}{3}$

8 $\dfrac{7}{10}$, $\dfrac{2}{3}$

9 $\dfrac{5}{7}$, $\dfrac{3}{5}$

_____

_____

_____

10 $\dfrac{7}{8}$, $\dfrac{8}{10}$

11 $\dfrac{7}{9}$, $\dfrac{4}{5}$

12 $\dfrac{3}{5}$, $\dfrac{5}{9}$

_____

_____

_____

4 Cancelling fractions

Sometimes a fraction can be written as an equivalent fraction with smaller numbers.

We call this writing as a **simpler fraction**, or as a fraction in its **lowest terms**.

To do this we use **cancelling**.

To cancel $\dfrac{9}{12}$ first find the highest common factor of 9 and 12: that is, 3.

Then divide:

$$\overset{\div\,3}{\underset{\div\,3}{\dfrac{9}{12}}} = \dfrac{3}{4} \quad \text{in its lowest terms}$$

To cancel $\dfrac{48}{64}$:

The highest common factor of 48 and 64 is 16.

Then divide:

$$\overset{\div\,16}{\underset{\div\,16}{\dfrac{48}{64}}} = \dfrac{3}{4}$$

Always check the final answer to see if it can be cancelled again!

Exercise 9:4

Cancel these fractions to their lowest terms.

1 $\dfrac{6}{8} =$ **2** $\dfrac{4}{14} =$ **3** $\dfrac{9}{12} =$ **4** $\dfrac{10}{15} =$

_____   _____   _____   _____

5 $\dfrac{5}{20} =$ **6** $\dfrac{21}{35} =$ **7** $\dfrac{8}{24} =$ **8** $\dfrac{24}{54} =$

_____   _____   _____   _____

9 $\dfrac{30}{36} =$ **10** $\dfrac{27}{45} =$ **11** $\dfrac{35}{49} =$ **12** $\dfrac{18}{24} =$

_____   _____   _____   _____

13 $\dfrac{54}{120} =$ **14** $\dfrac{36}{90} =$ **15** $\dfrac{54}{72} =$ **16** $\dfrac{48}{80} =$

_____   _____   _____   _____

PARENTS AND HELPERS

This is a good time to practise times tables.
A knowledge of times tables helps in finding numbers to cancel with.

5   Adding simple fractions

When the denominators are the same:

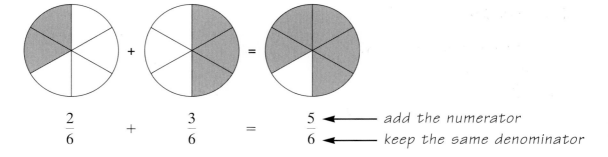

$$\dfrac{2}{6} \quad + \quad \dfrac{3}{6} \quad = \quad \dfrac{5}{6}$$ ← add the numerator
← keep the same denominator

When the denominators are different:
You need to change at least one of the fractions into an equivalent fraction.
We need the same denominators to add the fraction.

$$\dfrac{2}{3} + \dfrac{2}{9} \quad \boxed{\begin{array}{c} \times 3 \\ \curvearrowright \\ \dfrac{2}{3} = \dfrac{6}{9} \\ \curvearrowright \\ \times 3 \end{array}} \quad \dfrac{6}{9} + \dfrac{2}{9} = \dfrac{7}{9}$$

Sometimes you may be able to cancel
your answer into lower terms.

79

Exercise 9:5

Work out the answers as fractions in their lowest terms.

1 $\dfrac{2}{5} + \dfrac{2}{5} =$ _____

2 $\dfrac{1}{6} + \dfrac{4}{6} =$ _____

3 $\dfrac{3}{9} + \dfrac{4}{9} =$ _____

4 $\dfrac{2}{8} + \dfrac{3}{8} =$ _____

5 $\dfrac{3}{10} + \dfrac{5}{10} =$ _____

6 $\dfrac{4}{12} + \dfrac{5}{12} =$ _____

7 $\dfrac{3}{8} + \dfrac{1}{4} =$ _____

8 $\dfrac{1}{8} + \dfrac{5}{32} =$ _____

9 $\dfrac{1}{2} + \dfrac{3}{16} =$ _____

10 $\dfrac{5}{8} + \dfrac{1}{32} =$ _____

11 $\dfrac{1}{4} + \dfrac{3}{32} =$ _____

12 $\dfrac{7}{16} + \dfrac{1}{4} =$ _____

6 Subtracting simple fractions

When the denominators are the same:

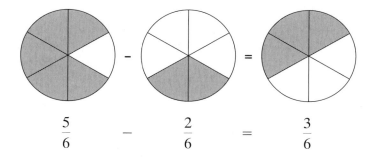

$$\frac{5}{6} \quad - \quad \frac{2}{6} \quad = \quad \frac{3}{6}$$

Note: $\frac{3}{6}$ is equivalent to $\frac{1}{2}$.

When the denominators are different:

You need to change at least one of the fractions into an equivalent fraction.
We need the same denominators to subtract the fraction.

$$\frac{3}{4} - \frac{5}{8} \qquad \boxed{\begin{array}{c} \times 2 \\ \frac{3}{4} = \frac{6}{8} \\ \times 2 \end{array}} \qquad \frac{6}{8} - \frac{5}{8} = \frac{1}{8}$$

Exercise 9:6

Work out the answers as fractions in their lowest terms.

1 $\dfrac{5}{6} - \dfrac{4}{6} =$

2 $\dfrac{6}{7} - \dfrac{4}{7} =$

_____   _____

3 $\dfrac{11}{12} - \dfrac{6}{12} =$

4 $\dfrac{8}{10} - \dfrac{5}{10} =$

_____

_____

5 $\dfrac{7}{8} - \dfrac{1}{4} =$

6 $\dfrac{5}{8} - \dfrac{1}{2} =$

_____

_____

7 $\dfrac{7}{8} - \dfrac{3}{16} =$

8 $\dfrac{15}{16} - \dfrac{3}{4} =$

_____

_____

9 $\dfrac{7}{8} - \dfrac{13}{16} =$

10 $\dfrac{5}{8} - \dfrac{1}{16} =$

_____

_____

11 $\dfrac{1}{4} - \dfrac{3}{16} =$

12 $\dfrac{3}{4} - \dfrac{7}{32} =$

_____

_____

Equivalence poster

It is helpful to have a poster that shows all the equivalent fractions.

For each fraction write down the first 9 equivalent fractions.

Write this information neatly on to a poster for display.

$\frac{1}{2}$									
$\frac{1}{3}$									
$\frac{1}{4}$									
$\frac{1}{5}$									
$\frac{1}{6}$									
$\frac{1}{7}$									
$\frac{1}{8}$									
$\frac{1}{9}$									
$\frac{1}{10}$									
$\frac{1}{11}$									
$\frac{1}{12}$									
$\frac{1}{13}$									
$\frac{1}{14}$									
$\frac{1}{15}$									
$\frac{1}{16}$									

10 Fractions – multiplication and division

1 Mixed numbers

Mixed numbers are numbers with a whole number part and a fraction part.

$5\frac{2}{3}$ is 5 whole ones and two thirds.

Improper fractions are fractions that are "top heavy".

$$\frac{13}{3}$$

Mixed numbers can be changed into improper fractions:

$5\frac{4}{7}$ is 5 whole ones and four sevenths.

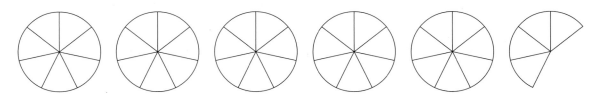

$$5 \text{ whole ones} = \frac{7}{7} + \frac{7}{7} + \frac{7}{7} + \frac{7}{7} + \frac{7}{7}$$

$$5\frac{4}{7} = \underbrace{\frac{7}{7} + \frac{7}{7} + \frac{7}{7} + \frac{7}{7} + \frac{7}{7}}_{5} + \overset{\frac{4}{7}}{\frac{4}{7}} = \frac{39}{7}$$

Exercise 10:1

Change these mixed numbers into improper fractions.

1 $3\frac{1}{2} = \frac{}{2}$ **2** $4\frac{2}{5} = \frac{}{5}$ **3** $2\frac{2}{3} = \frac{}{3}$ **4** $7\frac{3}{4} = \frac{}{4}$

5 $3\frac{7}{10} = \frac{}{10}$ **6** $2\frac{5}{6} = \frac{}{6}$ **7** $3\frac{3}{4} = \frac{}{4}$ **8** $9\frac{2}{3} = \frac{}{3}$

9 $4\frac{3}{5} = \frac{}{5}$ **10** $2\frac{5}{9} = \frac{}{9}$ **11** $5\frac{5}{10} = \frac{}{10}$ **12** $6\frac{2}{3} = \frac{}{3}$

13 $1\frac{3}{10} = \frac{}{10}$ **14** $5\frac{6}{7} = \frac{}{7}$ **15** $8\frac{5}{9} = \frac{}{9}$ **16** $5\frac{4}{5} = \frac{}{5}$

2 Improper fractions

Improper fractions are "top heavy" fractions.

$\dfrac{17}{3}$ is an improper fraction.

Mixed numbers are numbers with a whole number part and a fraction part.

$3\frac{4}{5}$ is 3 whole ones and four fifths.

Improper fractions can be changed into mixed numbers.

Method 1

$$\dfrac{13}{5} = \dfrac{5}{5} + \dfrac{5}{5} + \dfrac{3}{5} = 2\dfrac{3}{5}$$

$$\dfrac{26}{7} = \dfrac{7}{7} + \dfrac{7}{7} + \dfrac{7}{7} + \dfrac{5}{7} = 3\dfrac{5}{7}$$

Method 2

OR $\quad 13 \div 5 = 2 \text{ r } 3$ which is $2\dfrac{3}{5}$

OR $\quad 26 \div 7 = 3 \text{ r } 5$ which is $3\dfrac{5}{7}$

Exercise 10:2

Write these improper fractions as mixed fractions.

1 $\dfrac{7}{2} =$

2 $\dfrac{9}{4} =$

3 $\dfrac{10}{3} =$

4 $\dfrac{20}{9} =$

_____ _____ _____ _____

5 $\dfrac{22}{3} =$

6 $\dfrac{9}{8} =$

7 $\dfrac{32}{7} =$

8 $\dfrac{43}{6} =$

_____ _____ _____ _____

9 $\dfrac{44}{5} =$

10 $\dfrac{63}{10} =$

11 $\dfrac{43}{12} =$

12 $\dfrac{71}{8} =$

_____ _____ _____ _____

13 $\dfrac{62}{9} =$ _____

14 $\dfrac{47}{10} =$ _____

15 $\dfrac{61}{8} =$ _____

16 $\dfrac{25}{4} =$ _____

17 $\dfrac{37}{10} =$ _____

18 $\dfrac{41}{9} =$ _____

19 $\dfrac{53}{12} =$ _____

20 $\dfrac{49}{5} =$ _____

3 Ordering mixed numbers

To write mixed numbers in order:
1 put them in order of the whole numbers
2 put the mixed fractions with the same **whole** number in order of the fraction part.

Write in descending order: $3\frac{1}{4}$, $2\frac{2}{5}$, $3\frac{3}{8}$

Order by whole number:

$3\frac{1}{4}$, $3\frac{3}{8}$, $2\frac{2}{5}$ *Same whole number, order these next.*

Order by fraction part: change to the same denominator to compare size.

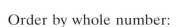

$\dfrac{1}{4} = \dfrac{2}{8}$, which is less than $\dfrac{3}{8}$

The final descending order is: $3\frac{3}{8}$, $3\frac{1}{4}$, $2\frac{2}{5}$

The ascending order would be: $2\frac{2}{5}$, $3\frac{1}{4}$, $3\frac{3}{8}$

Exercise 10:3

Write these fractions in descending order:

1 $2\frac{3}{8}$, $2\frac{4}{10}$

2 $5\frac{4}{5}$, $5\frac{5}{7}$

3 $4\frac{2}{5}$, $4\frac{3}{4}$

_____

_____

_____

4 $3\frac{7}{9}$, $3\frac{9}{10}$

5 $6\frac{1}{2}$, $6\frac{2}{7}$

6 $5\frac{5}{7}$, $5\frac{8}{12}$

_____

_____

_____

Write these fractions in ascending order:

7 $3\frac{7}{8}$, $2\frac{2}{3}$, $3\frac{4}{5}$

8 $5\frac{3}{10}$, $5\frac{2}{5}$, $4\frac{1}{3}$

_____

_____

9 $3\frac{4}{5}$, $4\frac{1}{3}$, $3\frac{5}{7}$

10 $6\frac{4}{7}$, $4\frac{3}{5}$, $6\frac{7}{9}$

_____

_____

PARENTS AND HELPERS

Another way of ordering mixed numbers is to write each mixed number on a card.

$3\frac{1}{4}$　　　$3\frac{3}{8}$　　　$2\frac{2}{5}$

Then write the equivalent fractions on the cards where necessary for comparison.

$3\frac{1}{4} = 3\frac{2}{8}$　　　$3\frac{3}{8} =$　　　$2\frac{2}{5} =$

Now rearrange the cards in the correct order.

4 Fractions of quantities

A fraction of a quantity is also a division of that quantity.
To find a fraction of a quantity we **divide.**

$\frac{1}{5}$ of 135g

$\frac{1}{5}$ of 135g means

135 divided into
five parts.

$135 \div 5 = 27g$

$\frac{2}{3}$ of £3.30

$\frac{1}{3}$ of £3.30 is £3.30 $\div$ 3 = £1.10

So $\frac{2}{3}$ is twice as much:
£1.10 $\times$ 2 = £2.2**0**

*Remember to keep the
nought for money.*

Exercise 10:4

Work out:

1 $\frac{1}{3}$ of £3.96

£ _____

2 $\frac{1}{4}$ of 884 km

_____ km

3 $\frac{1}{8}$ of 2568

_____

4 $\frac{2}{5}$ of £124

£ _____

5 $\frac{4}{9}$ of 38.25 kg

_____ kg

6 $\frac{3}{4}$ of 142 mm

_____ mm

7 $\frac{2}{3}$ of 2295 people

_____ people

8 $\frac{3}{8}$ of 19.68 m

_____ m

9 $\frac{7}{10}$ of 24 kg

_____ kg

10 $\frac{5}{6}$ of £7.38

£ _____

11 $\frac{3}{10}$ of 1350

_____

12 $\frac{5}{7}$ of £5271

£ _____

5 Writing parts as fractions

In a bag there are 12 black pens, 6 blue pens and 2 red pens.
What fraction of the pens are black?

The total number of pens is 12 + 6 + 2 = 20 pens
So the fraction that are black is 12/20 = 3/5

Cancel your answer to its simplest form.

Exercise 10:5

Write your fraction answer in its simplest form.

1 There are 20 chocolates in a box. 15 are left.
What fraction of the chocolates in the box have been eaten?

_____

2 Of 80 sheep in a field, 16 are black.
What fraction of the sheep are black?

_____

3 There is 400 ml of oil in a can. 120 ml is poured out.
What fraction remains?

_____

4 In one hour, 7 trains were on time, 5 were late and 4 were early.
What fraction of the trains were late?

_____

5 There are 63 passengers on a coach. 40 of them are female.
What fraction of the passengers are male?

_____

6 A store had 84 T-shirts in stock. 60 of them have been sold.
What fraction of the original stock is left?

_____

7 What fraction of the letters in MISSISSIPPI are letter I's?

_____

8 There are 108 days until Darren's birthday.
He will be at school for 48 of these days.
For what fraction of the days will he not be at school?

_____

9 On a shopping trip Jamila spent £20 on books,
£70 on clothes and £30 on CDs.
What fraction of her money did she spend on clothes?

_____

10 Of the 365 days in last year, Bob used his car
on 214 days to go to work, and on 88 days for pleasure.
For what fraction of the year was the car not used?

_____

6 Multiplying simple fractions

To multiply fractions we do **not** need the same denominators.
Cancel the answers into their simplest form.

$$\frac{3}{7} \times \frac{2}{7} = \frac{3 \times 2}{7 \times 6} = \frac{6}{42} = \frac{1}{7} \qquad \text{Cancel}$$

$$4 \times \frac{3}{8} = \frac{4}{1} \times \frac{3}{8} = \frac{12}{8} = 1\frac{4}{8} = 1\frac{1}{2} \qquad \text{Cancel}$$

Exercise 10:6

Show all your working and give your answers in their simplest form.

1 $\dfrac{4}{5} \times \dfrac{2}{3} =$

_____

2 $\dfrac{5}{6} \times \dfrac{5}{7} =$

_____

3 $\dfrac{1}{3} \times \dfrac{6}{7} =$

_____

4 $12 \times \dfrac{2}{3} =$

_____

5 $\dfrac{4}{5} \times \dfrac{10}{7} =$

_____

6 $\dfrac{4}{5} \times \dfrac{10}{12} =$

_____

7 $20 \times \dfrac{5}{8} =$

_____

8 $\dfrac{9}{10} \times \dfrac{11}{18} =$

_____

ACTIVITY

What is half of a half?

What is a quarter of a quarter?

Are these the results that you might have expected?

Find other fractions of fractions. Write down all your results.

7 Dividing simple fractions

To divide fractions we use two operations together:

Division is the inverse (opposite) of multiplication.

$$\frac{5}{9} \div \frac{5}{6}$$

becomes

A fraction written upside down is the inverse (opposite) fraction.

$$\frac{5}{9} \times \frac{6}{5} = \frac{30}{45} = \frac{2}{3}$$

$$\frac{7}{8} \div 3 = \frac{7}{8} \div \frac{3}{1}$$

becomes

$$\frac{7}{8} \times \frac{1}{3} = \frac{7}{24}$$

Exercise 10:7

Show all your working and give your answers in their simplest form.

1 $\dfrac{1}{2} \div \dfrac{2}{3} =$

2 $\dfrac{1}{6} \div \dfrac{2}{3} =$

3 $\dfrac{3}{8} \div \dfrac{2}{3} =$

_____

4 $\dfrac{4}{9} \div 5 =$

_____

5 $\dfrac{6}{7} \div \dfrac{3}{5} =$

_____

6 $\dfrac{7}{10} \div 3 =$

_____

7 $\dfrac{5}{12} \div \dfrac{1}{6} =$

_____

8 $\dfrac{3}{8} \div \dfrac{1}{4} =$

_____

1 Fraction divisions

What is a half divided by a half?

What is a third divided by a third?

What is a quarter divided by a quarter?

Can you explain your answers?

Can you predict what the answer will be for any fraction divided by itself?

2 Fractions of £1

£1 can be divided up many different ways.

$\frac{1}{2}$ of £1 is 50p

$\frac{1}{5}$ of £1 is 20p

Find:

a $\frac{1}{3}$ of £1

b $\frac{1}{4}$ of £1

c $\frac{1}{6}$ of £1

What do you notice from your answers?

Find all the possible ways of dividing £1 that will give you a whole number of pence as your answer.

3   Fractions of a circle

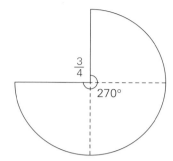

a A circle has 360°. It can be divided up in very many ways because 360 has many factors.

The table shows some of the fractions of 360°.

Fraction	$\frac{1}{2}$	$\frac{1}{3}$	$\frac{1}{4}$	$\frac{1}{5}$	$\frac{1}{6}$	$\frac{1}{7}$	$\frac{1}{8}$	$\frac{1}{9}$	$\frac{1}{10}$
Angle	180°	120°	90°						

Complete the table, filling in the angles that are a whole number of degrees.

b List all the other fractions that give you angles that are whole numbers of degrees:

_____

c For each fraction in the table, draw a small circle and shade that fraction. Label with the size of the angle and the fraction of the circle.

11 Ratios

1 Simplifying ratios

Ratios are simplified in the same way as fractions, by cancelling the numbers.
The quantities must have the same units. If not, you must change them all
into the same units before simplifying.

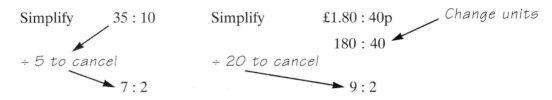

Simplify   35 : 10   Simplify   £1.80 : 40p   *Change units*

                                                      180 : 40

÷ 5 to cancel   *÷ 20 to cancel*

                  7 : 2   9 : 2

Exercise 11.1

Write these ratios in their simplest form.

1   6 : 8   **2**   36 : 6   **3**   12 : 48

_____   _____   _____

4   8 m : 4 m   **5**   6 g : 18 g   **6**   3 : 15

_____   _____   _____

7   1 mm : 1 cm   **8**   3 min : 1 hour   **9**   60p : £1.60

_____   _____   _____

10   4 days : 2 weeks   **11**   2 mm : 1 cm   **12**   30 min : 2 hours

_____   _____   _____

13   50p : £3   **14**   250 g : 1 kg   **15**   8 mm : 3 cm

_____   _____   _____

ACTIVITY

Take 24 counters (or other objects) and divide them into 2 piles in the ratio 1 : 3.
What other ratios can you represent with 24 counters?
What ratios can you represent with 3 piles of counters?

2 Unitary ratios

In a unitary ratio, one of the quantities is 1.

It takes 80 minutes for Tom to row 4 times across a lake.
Find how long it takes Tom to make 1 journey across the lake.
    4 crossings = 80 minutes
    1 crossing = 80 ÷ 4 = 20 minutes

Exercise 11.2

1 Peaches cost 84p for 6.
How much does one peach cost?

_____ p

2 A book with 495 pages is 15 mm thick.
How many pages are there per 1 mm?

_____

3 It takes 20 minutes to empty a tank containing 280 litres of water.
How much water is emptied per minute?

_____ litres

4 A lorry uses 8 litres of diesel to travel 120 km.
How far does it travel on 1 litre?

_____ km

5 6 bags of sand cost £27.
What is the cost of one bag?

£ _____

6 Rajesh cycles 112 metres in 35 seconds.
How far does he cycle per second?

_____ m

7   8 tubes of toothpaste weigh a total of 976 g.
How much does one tube of toothpaste weigh?

_____ g

8   A hot air balloon rose 640 metres
steadily in 16 minutes.
How far did it rise each minute?

_____ m

3   Direct proportion

In 6 minutes a machine punches out 48 metal parts.
How many would it punch out in 5 minutes?
      In 6 minutes 48 parts are punched
      In 1 minute 48 ÷ 6 = 8 parts are punched
      In 5 minutes 8 × 5 = 40 parts are punched

Exercise 11.3

Assume that all rates remain constant.

1   4 tubes of sweets cost 84p.
How much do 3 tubes cost?

_____ p

2   7 CDs cost £63.
How much will 12 CDs cost?

£ _____

3   A car uses 8 litres of petrol to travel 104 km.
How far will it travel on 11 litres of petrol?

_____ km

4   6 identical boxes have a total weight of 27 kg.
What is the weight of just 5 boxes?

_____ kg

5   3 kg of rice costs £3.60.
How much does 4 kg cost?

£ _____

6 Melanie walks 2 miles in 46 minutes.
How long would it take her to walk 3 miles?

_____ min

7 7 identical envelopes weigh 224 g in total.
How much do just 6 of the envelopes weigh?

_____ g

8 A car travels 630 miles in 14 hours at a steady speed.
How far will the car have travelled in 17 hours?

_____ miles

4 Inverse proportion

4 machines take 5 days to produce enough parts for an order.
The following week there is an identical order for parts.
How long will it take 10 machines to do the job?

First find how much work it would have been for one machine:

$4 \times 5 = 20$ days' work for 1 machine

For 10 machines it would take $20 \div 10 = 2$ days.

Exercise 11.4

Assume all rates remain constant.

1 Chocolate boxes are packed in 7 crates each holding 12 boxes.
The same boxes are re-packed into 6 larger crates.
How many boxes are packed in each crate?

_____

2 A supermarket shelf holds 18 cereal packets, each 6 cm wide.
The cereal boxes are replaced with 12 new packets with
the same total width.
What is the width of each new box?

_____ cm

3 6 machines can fill an order in 4 days. For another order
of the same size 8 machines are used.
How long will it take them?

_____ days

4 There are two ponds in a garden.
Both the ponds are the same size.
4 pipes fill the first pond in 12 minutes.
How long will it take to fill the second pond using just 3 pipes?

_____ min

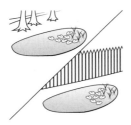

5 If I spend £15 a day, my holiday cash will last for 14 days.
How long will it last if I spend £10.50 per day?

_____ days

6 A sack of dog food feeds 6 dogs for 10 days.
For how many days will an identical sack
of food feed 4 dogs?

_____ days

7 A train travels at 30 km/h for 3 hours.
How long will a faster train take to make the
same journey at a speed of 60 km/h?

_____ h

8 Two men can paint a room in 120 minutes.
How long will it take 3 men to paint another
room of the same size?

_____ min

5 Using ratios

Two lengths are in the ratio 3 : 4.
The longer length is 20 cm.
Find the smaller length.

	Smaller	:	Larger		
	3	:	4		
		:	20	× 5	*20 ÷ 4 = 5 as a multiplier*
3 × 5 =	15 cm	:	20 cm		

Exercise 11:5

Change the recipes for the number shown.

1 Cassoulet (for 4 people)
Change for 6 people

haricot beans	350 g	_____ g
onions	2	_____
bacon	100 g	_____ g
chicken drumsticks	4	_____
stock	900 ml	_____ ml

2 Rock cakes (8 cakes)
Change for 20 cakes

self-raising flour	250 g	_____ g
margarine	150 g	_____ g
demerara sugar	80 g	_____ g
mixed dried fruit	150 g	_____ g
milk (tablespoons)	2	_____
eggs	2	_____

Answer these questions.

3 On a supermarket shelf the ratio of butter tubs to
margarine tubs is 3 : 7. There are 18 tubs of butter.
How many tubs of margarine are there?

_____

4　In a class the ratio of boys to girls is 1 : 2.
There are 9 boys in the class.
How many girls are there?

_____

5　In an animal sanctuary the ratio of cats to dogs is 5 : 6.
There are 25 cats.
How many dogs are there?

_____

6　On a farm the number of cows to sheep is in the ratio 2 : 5.
There are 45 sheep.
How many cows are there?

_____

PARENTS AND HELPERS

Give students recipe books and ask them to write out recipes for different numbers of people.

This should also lead to a discussion about rounding. For example, what to do when you need $\frac{3}{4}$ of an egg?

6　Dividing in ratios

An amount of £30.24 is divided between two children in the ratio 3 : 4.
How much does each receive?

$$3 : 4 \rightarrow 7 \text{ parts}$$

£30.24 ÷ 7 = 4.32 per part

One child gets 3 × £4.32 = £12.96

The other gets 4 × £4.32 = £17.28

Check: £12.96 + £17.28 = £30.24

Exercise 11.6

1　Divide £12.40 in the ratio 2 : 3

£ _____ , £ _____

2　Divide 24.8 litres in the ratio 3 : 5

_____ litres, _____ litres

3   Divide 30.78 metres in the ratio 4 : 5

_____ m, _____ m

4   Divide 38 kg in the ratio 3 : 5

_____ kg, _____ kg

5   The ratio of boys to girls
in the class is 3 : 4.
There are 28 pupils in the class.
Find the numbers of boys and
girls in the class.

_____ boys, _____ girls

6   Jill and Jenny share £6.50
in the ratio 1 : 4
How much does each receive?

£ _____ , £ _____

7   On a shelf there are 945 tins of paint.
The ratio of white tins to coloured tins is 2 : 5.
How many white tins are there?

_____ white tins

8   At a party the ratio of tumblers
to wine glasses is 3 : 4.
The total number of wine glasses
and tumblers is 119.
How many wine glasses are there?

_____ glasses

1 Recipes

Find some recipes in a cookbook.
Write out the list of ingredients and the quantities needed.
Re-write the recipe for
a double the quantity
b treble the quantity
c half the quantity

2 Mixing concrete

Concrete is mixed from cement, sand and stone. The quantities mixed depend on what the concrete is used for.

The table shows the quantities to mix for building foundations and paths. All quantities are in kilograms.

	Cement	Sand	Stone
Foundation	1	2	4
Paths	1	2	3

Complete the tables below to show the quantities needed.

Foundations

Cement	1	2	3					20
Sand	2			10		20		
Stone	4				32		48	

Paths

Cement	1	2	4					
Sand	2			10	16			
Stone	3					33	48	60

12 Percentages

1 Recognising percentages

A percentage is a fraction of 100.

There are 100 squares in this grid.

65 of them are shaded.

This shows $\frac{65}{100}$ or 65%.

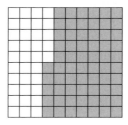

Exercise 12:1

Write down the percentage of each grid that is shaded.

1
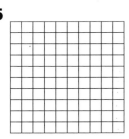

_____ %

2
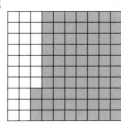

_____ %

3
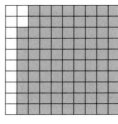

_____ %

4
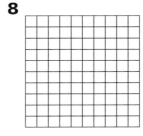

_____ %

Shade each diagram to represent the percentage that is shown.

5
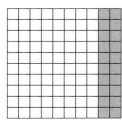

10 %

6
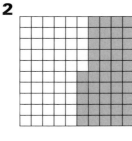

75 %

7
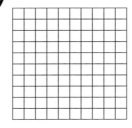

48 %

8
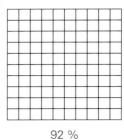

63 %

9
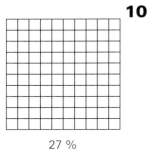

27 %

10
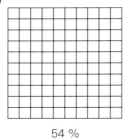

54 %

11
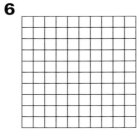

38 %

12
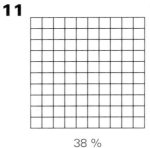

92 %

2   Estimating percentages

100% represents a whole.

This circle represents 100%:

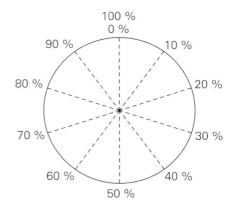

Common percentages are:

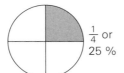 $\frac{1}{4}$ or 25 %

 $\frac{1}{2}$ or 50 %

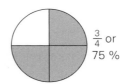 $\frac{3}{4}$ or 75 %

We can estimate the percentage of circles that are shaded.

More than $\frac{1}{4}$ or 25%   between 30% and
Less than $\frac{1}{2}$ or 50%   40% but nearer 40%

A good estimate would be about 38%

Exercise 12:2

Estimate the percentage shaded.

1   **2**   **3**   **4**

_____ %   _____ %   _____ %   _____ %

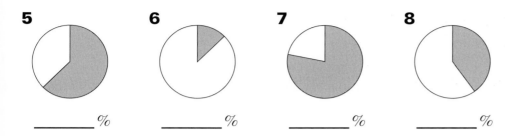

5	6	7	8
_____ %	_____ %	_____ %	_____ %

Shade each circle to show the percentage.

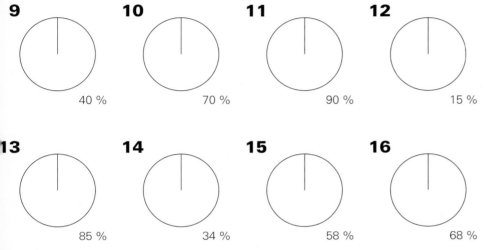

9	10	11	12
40 %	70 %	90 %	15 %

13	14	15	16
85 %	34 %	58 %	68 %

3   Conversion from percentages

To change a percentage to a fraction, write the percentage as a fraction of 100:

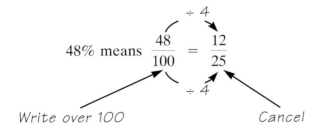

$$48\% \text{ means } \frac{48}{100} = \frac{12}{25}$$

Write over 100   *Cancel*

To change a percentage to a decimal, divide by 100:

82% means $82 \div 100 = 0.82$ as a decimal.

Exercise 12:3

Complete the table:

Percentage	Fraction	Decimal	Percentage	Fraction	Decimal
3%			32%		
16%			41%		
77%			68%		
80%			20%		
51%			72%		
10%			33%		
45%			49%		
38%			36%		

PARENTS AND HELPERS

It is helpful to see percentages in real life. They are frequently used in articles in magazines, newspapers, or on the television.

Collect cuttings and notes on percentages and how they are used, and make a notebook or scrapbook of them.

4 Conversion to percentages

To change a decimal to a percentage, multiply by 100:

0.37 to a percentage is $0.37 \times 100 = 37\%$

To change a fraction to a percentage multiply by $\dfrac{100}{1}$ and cancel if possible.

$\dfrac{9}{20}$ to a percentage is $\dfrac{9}{20} \times \dfrac{100}{1} = \dfrac{900}{20} = 45\%$

Exercise 12:4

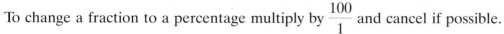

Change these into percentages.

1 $\dfrac{9}{50}$

_____ %

2 0.35

_____ %

3 $\dfrac{11}{20}$

_____ %

4 0.2

_____ %

5 $\dfrac{7}{10}$

_____ %

6 $\dfrac{2}{5}$

_____ %

7 0.08

_____ %

8 $\dfrac{7}{25}$

_____ %

9 0.1

_____ %

10 $\dfrac{24}{25}$

_____ %

11 $\dfrac{13}{20}$

_____ %

12 0.83

_____ %

5 Sum to 100%

When something is divided into percentage parts, all of those parts should sum to 100%.

The passengers on a train have all bought saver, standard or first class tickets. 40% have bought saver tickets and 35% have bought standard tickets.

What percentage have bought first class tickets?

$40\% + 35\% = 75\%$
$100\% - 75\% = 25\%$
25% have bought first class tickets

Exercise 12:5

1   For 10% of the days on holiday it rained.
On what percentage of the days didn't it rain?

_____ %

2   In a cookbook 45% of the pictures are black and white.
What percentage of the pictures are colour?

_____ %

3   There are cats and dogs at a pet sanctuary.
60% of the pets are dogs.
What percentage are cats?

_____ %

4   In a survey of people travelling to France,
10% went by plane, and 25% by the channel tunnel.
What percentage went to France by ferry?

_____ %

5   In a music shop 30% of people bought tapes.
What percentage of people did **not** buy a tape?

_____ %

6   65% of the people on a train are travelling to work.
What percentage are **not** travelling to work?

_____ %

7   A box contains red, blue and black pens.
15% of the pens are red, and 40% are blue.
What percentage are black?

_____ %

8   55% of the passengers on a bus are adult male,
and 25% are adult female.
What percentage of the passengers are children?

_____ %

6   Percentages of quantities

Finding a percentage of a quantity is the same as finding a fraction of
quantity.

To find 43% of £20

$$\frac{43}{100} \times 20 = \frac{860}{100} = 8.6$$

Remember we are working with money, so the answer must be written
correctly as money.

$$8.6 \to £8.60$$

Exercise 12:6

1   Find 20% of 140 metres.

_____ m

2   Find 60% of £75.

£ _____

3   Find 35% of 60 km.

_____ km

4 Find 8% of 6400 g.

_____ g

5 35% of the money raised at a car boot sale is given to charity.
£200 is raised.
How much is given to charity?

£ _____

6 A metal cube weighs 800 g.
It is made of 60% copper and 40% brass.
What weight of copper is there in the metal cube?

_____ g

7 A piece of wood is 18 m long.
30% of the length is cut off.
Find the length of the piece cut off.

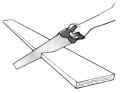

_____ m

8 7% of the bolts made by a machine are faulty.
3600 bolts have been made.
How many are faulty?

_____

7 Percentage increase and decrease

Quantities can increase or decrease by a percentage.

The price of a car originally costing £9500 is increased by 8%.
What is the new price of the car?

$$8\% \text{ of } £9500 \text{ is } \frac{8}{100} \times 9500 = \frac{76\,000}{100} = £760 \text{ (increase)}$$

So £9500 + £760 = £10 260

Make sure you add the increase on to the original amount.

Exercise 12:7

1 Increase £600 by 35%

£ _____

2 Increase 820 g by 7%

_____ g

3 Decrease 2500 m by 4%

_____ m

4 Decrease 90 kg by 15%

_____ kg

5 A computer originally costs £800. Its value falls by 35%.
What is its new value?

£ _____

6 An old piano is bought for £600.
Its value increases by 24% and it is then sold.
For what price is it sold?

£ _____

7 A piece of cheese weighing 5 kg has 15% cut off.
What is the new weight?

_____ kg

8 A tank contains 800 litres of water.
The amount of water in the tank is increased by 38%.
How much water is in the tank now?

_____ litres

PARENTS AND HELPERS

It is useful to compare the answer with the original quantity to see whether the
answer makes sense. An increase should make a quantity larger; a decrease should make
a quantity smaller.

8 Writing as percentages

Percentages are used to make comparisons, or to change figures into a more easily understood form.

Jonathan's French mark was 48 out of 60, and his English mark was 9 out of 15.
Which was his best result?

To compare the marks, write them as percentages.

$$\text{French: } 48 \text{ out of } 60 = \frac{48}{60} \rightarrow \frac{48}{60} \times 100 = \frac{4800}{60} = 80\%$$

$$\text{English: } 9 \text{ out of } 15 = \frac{9}{15} \rightarrow \frac{9}{15} \times 100 = \frac{900}{15} = 60\%$$

The French mark was his best result.

Exercise 12:8

1 Shahzad gains 7 marks out of 25 in a test.
Write this result as a percentage.

_____ %

2 3 toasters out of a batch of 20 are faulty.
What percentage of the toasters are faulty?

_____ %

3 Write 5p as a percentage of £2.

_____ %

4 168 litres of oil are removed from a tank containing 400 litres.
What percentage of the oil in the tank is removed?

_____ %

5 Of 200 bananas in a crate, 62 are already ripe.
What percentage of the bananas are ripe?

_____ %

6 Over a period of 50 days, the temperature dropped
below freezing on 31 days.
For what percentage of the days did the
temperature drop below zero?

_____ %

7 Of the 25 passengers on a bus, 23 were adults.
What percentage of the passengers were children?

_____ %

8 Amy had 13/20 in English, and 14/25 in Maths.
Write these marks as percentages.

_____ %, _____ %

9 Percentage fractions

To convert a percentage into a decimal or a fraction, divide by 100:

$4\frac{1}{2}\%$ becomes 4.5%. As a decimal: $4.5 \div 100 = 0.045$

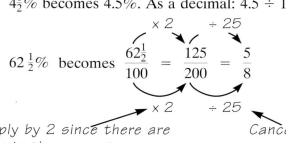

$62\frac{1}{2}\%$ becomes $\dfrac{62\frac{1}{2}}{100} = \dfrac{125}{200} = \dfrac{5}{8}$

×2 ÷25

Multiply by 2 since there are halves in the percentage.   Cancel

To calculate with a fractional percentage, change it into an equivalent fraction, as above.

Find the VAT on a £220 CD player.
VAT is $17\frac{1}{2}\%$.

$$17\frac{1}{2}\% \text{ of } £220 = \frac{17\frac{1}{2}}{100} \times 220 = \frac{35}{200} \times 220 = \frac{7700}{200} = £38.50 \text{ VAT}$$

The VAT is £38.50

EXAMPLE

Exercise 12:9

Change these percentages to fractions.

1 $32\frac{1}{2}\%$

_____

2 $87\frac{1}{2}\%$

_____

3 $77\frac{1}{4}\%$

_____

4 $4\frac{3}{4}\%$

_____

Change these percentages to decimals.

5 $42\frac{1}{2}\%$ **6** $15\frac{1}{2}\%$ **7** $8\frac{1}{4}\%$ **8** $2\frac{3}{4}\%$

_____   _____   _____   _____

Change to a percentage:

9 $\frac{5}{8}$ **10** 0.055 **11** $\frac{7}{200}$

_____ %   _____ %   _____ %

12 0.445 **13** 0.625 **14** $\frac{5}{16}$

_____ %   _____ %   _____ %

15 Barbara's £14 000 salary is increased by $4\frac{1}{2}\%$.
What is the increase in Barbara's salary?

£ _____

16 A television costs £400 plus VAT at $17\frac{1}{2}\%$.
What is the cost of the television including VAT?

£ _____

17 A suit is advertised at a reduction of $12\frac{1}{2}\%$
from its normal price of £200.
What is the sale price of the suit?

£ _____

18 An electricity bill of £180 is reduced by $5\frac{1}{2}\%$.
How much is the reduced bill?

£ _____

19 The value of a £80 000 house increases by $3\frac{1}{2}\%$.
Calculate the new value of the house.

£ _____

20 The capacity of a football stadium is increased
by $17\frac{1}{2}\%$ from 20 000.
What is the new capacity of the stadium?

_____

Double your money

John has £1000 in the bank. The interest rate is 5%.
At the end of each year the interest for the account is calculated and added to the amount in his account.

For the first year: $£1000 \times \dfrac{5}{100} = £50$ interest

　　　　　Total amount is now £1000 + £50 = £1050

For the second year: $£1050 \times \dfrac{5}{100} = £52.50$ interest

　　　　　Total amount is now £1050 + £52.50 = £1102.50

For the third year: $£1102.50 \times \dfrac{5}{100} = 55.125$ (needs rounding)

　　　　　　　　　　　　　　 $= £55.13$ interest.

　　　　　Total amount is now £1102.50 + £55.13 = £1157.63

Year	1	2	3	4	5
Interest	£50	£52.50	£55.13		
Total	£1050	£1102.50	1157.63		

a　How many years does it take John to double his money?
　　John would have to get more than £2000 in his account.
　　Copy and complete the table to show how it is done.
　　You may need to add more columns.

b　What about different interest rates?
　　If the interest rate falls to 4% how long will it take to double the money?

c　Which doubles the money faster – a lower interest rate, or a higher interest rate?

d　What about different amounts?
　　If John had more money he would have to receive more money to double it.
　　If John starts with £2000, how long will it take him to double this to £4000 with an interest rate of 5%?

e　What about other larger amounts of money?
　　Does more starting money mean a longer or shorter time before the money is doubled?

13 Measurement

1 Temperature

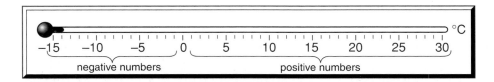

This is a thermometer. Thermometers are used to measure temperature.
The temperature can sometimes be **less than** zero.

The temperature falls 2°C from −1°C. The new temperature is −3°C.
A temperature change from −3°C to 4°C is a rise of 7 degrees.

Exercise 13:1

1　The temperature rose 6°C from −4°C.
　　What is the new temperature? 　　　　　　　　　　　　＿＿＿＿ °C

2　The temperature changes from −8°C to −2°C.
　　By how many degrees has it changed? 　　　　　　　　＿＿＿＿ °C

3　The temperature falls 4°C from −1°C.
　　What is the new temperature? 　　　　　　　　　　　　＿＿＿＿ °C

4　What is the difference in temperature between
　　−4°C and 3°C? 　　　　　　　　　　　　　　　　　　＿＿＿＿ °C

5　The temperature was −9°C. It rose by 6°C.
　　What is the new temperature? 　　　　　　　　　　　　＿＿＿＿ °C

6　The temperature fell 7°C from 2°C.
　　What is the new temperature? 　　　　　　　　　　　　＿＿＿＿ °C

7　The temperature rose 10°C from −5°C.
　　What is the new temperature? 　　　　　　　　　　　　＿＿＿＿ °C

8　What is the difference in temperature between
　　−9°C and 8°C? 　　　　　　　　　　　　　　　　　　＿＿＿＿ °C

2 Calendars

On page 161 you will find some details of units of time, in particular details of years, weeks and days. You need to know this information.

Here is part of the calendar for 2002.

January 2002

S	M	T	W	T	F	S
		1	2	3	4	5
6	7	8	9	10	11	12
13	14	15	16	17	18	19
20	21	22	23	24	25	26
27	28	29	30	31		

February 2002

S	M	T	W	T	F	S
					1	2
3	4	5	6	7	8	9
10	11	12	13	14	15	16
17	18	19	20	21	22	23
24	25	26	27	28		

March 2002

S	M	T	W	T	F	S
					1	2
3	4	5	6	7	8	9
10	11	12	13	14	15	16
17	18	19	20	21	22	23
24	25	26	27	28	29	30
31						

April 2002

S	M	T	W	T	F	S
	1	2	3	4	5	6
7	8	9	10	11	12	13
14	15	16	17	18	19	20
21	22	23	24	25	26	27
28	29	30				

May 2002

S	M	T	W	T	F	S
			1	2	3	4
5	6	7	8	9	10	11
12	13	14	15	16	17	18
19	20	21	22	23	24	25
26	27	28	29	30	31	

June 2002

S	M	T	W	T	F	S
						1
2	3	4	5	6	7	8
9	10	11	12	13	14	15
16	17	18	19	20	21	22
23	24	25	26	27	28	29
30						

a How many days are there after 21st February up to and including 5th March?

February   March

㉑ 22 23 24 25 26 27 28 1 2 3 4 5

Start counting after the first date   *12 days up to and including the second date.*

b What is the date on the second Tuesday of July?

Count the days into July:

June   July
S M T W T F S S M T
30 1 2 3 4 5 6 7 8 9

The second Tuesday of July is 9th July.

Exercise 13:2

Use the calendar for 2002 to answer these questions.

1 What date is the third Monday in February?

_____

2 What was the year 3 centuries before 2010?

_____

3 What is the date 20 days before April 5th?

_____

4 How many days are there after 22nd May up to and including 22nd June?

_____

5 What is the date exactly 7 weeks before 13th June?

_____

6 What day was Christmas Day in the year 2001?

_____

7 What is the date on the third Monday of July?

_____

8 How many days are there after 16th January up to and including 14th March?

_____

PARENTS AND HELPERS

Practice should be given in using the calendars for the current year.

How many days to your birthday?

How many days to the end of this month?

How many days to the end of the year?

How many days are there between the birthdays of your family members?

3　Time

On page 161 you will find some details of units of time, in particular details of the hours and minutes in a day. You need to know this information.

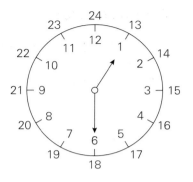

The time on this clock shows half past one.

The time can also be written:

	12-hour clock	24-hour clock
Morning	1.30 am	0130 h
Afternoon	1.30 pm	1330 h

Exercise 13:3

Change these 12-hour clock times to 24-hour clock times.

1 7.25 am 　 **2** 9.50 pm 　 **3** 10.10 am 　 **4** 11.30 pm

_____ h 　 _____ h 　 _____ h 　 _____ h

Change these 24-hour clock times to 12-hour clock times.

5 0222 h 　 **6** 2342 h 　 **7** 1050 h 　 **8** 1304 h

_____ 　 _____ 　 _____ 　 _____

Write the time in the 12-hour or the 24-hour clock to match the question.

9 $1\frac{1}{2}$ hours before 9.40 pm 　　　　 **10** $2\frac{1}{4}$ hours before 0320 h.

_____ 　　　　　　　　　　　 _____

11 $3\frac{3}{4}$ hours after 1535 h 　　　　 **12** $1\frac{3}{4}$ hours after 11.45 am

_____ 　　　　　　　　　　　 _____

Work out how long it is between these times.

13   1610 h to 1845 h

_____

14   3.40 pm to 4.55 pm

_____

15   9.30 am to 2.50 pm

_____

16   0425 h to 2215 h

_____

PARENTS AND HELPERS

Practice at using both 12- and 24-hour clocks is essential. Try not to rely on digital clocks, as clocks with circular faces are still in common use. Practice could involve: planning cooking times, finding out the times of television programmes, calculating the length of video tapes needed for a sequence of programmes, or programming the video recorder.

4   Timetables

We can use timetables to plan journeys.
Timetables use 24-hour clock times.
This is a train timetable between Blackpool North and Manchester Airport:

Blackpool North		1827		1900	2000		2100	2200	
Preston	1754		1854	1917	2028	2043	2105	2127	2227
Chorley	1807		1907		2041	2056	2116	2140	2240
Blackrod	1815		1915		2049			2148	2248
Lostock	1820		1920		2053	2115	2125	2153	2253
Bolton	1825		1925	1943	2100	2123	2130	2200	2300
Salford Crescent		1939		2013	2113	2146	2213	2213	2313
Deansgate	1842		1942		2116	2149			2316
Manchester Oxford Rd	1859	1945	1959	2019	2119			2219	2319
Manchester Piccadilly	1903	1949	2003	2023	2123			2223	2331
Heald Green					2136			2238	2351
Manchester Airport	1922		2022	2042	2142			2244	2357

Exercise 13:4

1 What is the maximum number of stations a train could stop at between Chorley and Deansgate?

_____

2 At what time does the 2028 from Preston arrive at Manchester Airport?

_____

3 How long does it take the 2148 from Blackrod to get to Salford Crescent?

_____

4 A train arrives at Manchester Piccadilly at 1949.
At what time did it leave Blackpool?

_____

5 How long does it take the 2041 from Chorley to get to Manchester Oxford Road?

_____

6 You need to meet a friend at Deansgate by 2200.
What is the latest time you could catch a train from Lostock?

_____

7 You need to be at Manchester Airport by 2300.
What is the latest time you could catch a train from Preston?

_____

8 You need to be at Salford Crescent between 2000 and 2200.
Which trains from Blackpool would get you there between these times?

_____

PARENTS AND HELPERS

Planning a journey using local bus and train timetables gives useful practice in reading timetables.

5 Taking measurements

The metric units you need to know are listed on page 161.

You should be able to use a range of measuring instruments.
The most common is the ruler, for measuring lengths.

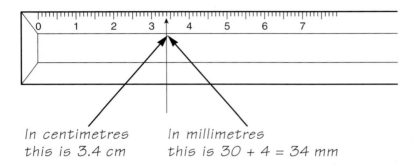

In centimetres
this is 3.4 cm

In millimetres
this is 30 + 4 = 34 mm

Exercise 13:5

Measure these lines. Give your answer in centimetres, as a decimal if appropriate.
Write your answer on the line.

1 _____

2 _____

3 _____

4 _____

5 _____

6 _____

Measure these lines, giving your answer in millimetres.
Write your answer on the line.

7 _____

8 _____

9 _____

10 _____

11 _____

12 _____

Write down the metric unit you would use to make each measurement:

13   the volume of milk in a carton   _____

14   the weight of this book   _____   **15**   the length of a garden   _____

16   the width of a pencil   _____   **17**   your own weight   _____

18   the length of your arm   _____

6   Metric units

The metric units you need to know are listed on page 161.

To change a small unit to a larger unit: **divide**.
To change a large unit to a smaller unit: **multiply**.

EXAMPLE

a To change 1.3 kg into g.
   large unit → smaller unit so **multiply**.
      1.3 × 1000 = 1300 g

Conversion factor:
1 kg = 1000 g

b A nail is 5 cm long. 1200 nails are laid end to end.
   What is the total length in metres?
      5 × 1200 = 6000 cm
   Then change to metres: 6000 ÷ 100 = 60 m

Exercise 13:6

Change the following:

1   9 cm into mm   **2**   55 mg into g   **3**   6 m into cm

_____ mm   _____ g   _____ cm

4   0.2 litres into ml   **5**   38 km into m   **6**   1700 ml into litres

_____ ml   _____ m   _____ litres

7   534 cm into m   **8**   3560 g into kg   **9**   0.8 t into kg

_____ m   _____ kg   _____ kg

10   1.9 kg into g   **11**   0.05 litres into ml   **12**   7000 mm into m

_____ g   _____ ml   _____ m

13   A glass can hold 350 ml of water.
How many glasses can be filled from a
$1\frac{1}{2}$ litre bottle of water?

_____

14   A lorry carries a $2\frac{1}{2}$ tonne load of sand, which is to be packed
into 30 kg sacks.
How many sacks can be filled from the load of sand?

_____

15   500 rulers, each of length 30 cm, are to be laid end to end.
What is the total length in metres?

_____ m

7   Imperial units

The imperial units that you need to know are listed on page 161.

To change a small unit to a larger unit: **divide**.
To change a large unit to a smaller unit: **multiply**.

EXAMPLE

a Change 30 inches into feet and inches.
small units → large units so **divide**.
$30 \div 12 = 2$ r $6 = 2$ ft 6 in

Conversion factor:
12 in = 1 ft

b Change 3 st 4 lb into lbs.
large units → small units so **multiply**.
3 st 4 lb = (3×14) lb + 4 lb
         = 42 + 4 = 46 lbs

Conversion factor:
14 lb = 1 st

Exercise 13:7

Change the following:

1 50 in into ft and in

_____ ft _____ in

2 7 yd into ft

_____ ft

3 125 lb into st and lb

_____ st _____ lb

4 2 lb 3 oz into oz

_____ oz

5 $1\frac{1}{2}$ gal into pt

_____ pt

6 $\frac{1}{2}$ lb into oz

_____ oz

7 70 in into ft and in

_____ ft _____ in

8 80 fl oz into pt

_____ pt

9 200 lb into st and lb

_____ st _____ lb

10 3 ft 3 in into in

_____ in

11 3 lb 3 oz into oz

_____ oz

12 22 pt into gal and pt

_____ gal _____ pt

13 $12\frac{1}{2}$ st into lb

_____ lb

14 $6\frac{1}{2}$ ft into in

_____ in

15 3 pt into fl oz

_____ fl oz

16 1 yd 2 ft into ft

_____ ft

8 Imperial/metric equivalents

Two measurements that are approximately the same are said to be **equivalent** (≈).

The approximate imperial/metric equivalents you need to know are listed on page 161.

To change 56 kilometres into miles:

Use 1 km ≈ $\frac{5}{8}$ miles, or × $\frac{5}{8}$ for kilometres → miles

$56 \times \frac{5}{8} \approx \frac{280}{8} = 35$ miles

To change 12.5 cm into inches:

Use 1 in ≈ 2.5 cm, or ÷ 2.5 for in → cm

12.5 ÷ 2.5 = 5 inches.

Exercise 13:8

Change into approximate equivalents:

1 12 in into cm

_____ cm

2 $3\frac{1}{2}$ yd into metres

_____ m

3 30 kg into lb

_____ lb

4 8 litres into pints

_____ pt

5 4 ft into cm

_____ cm

6 18 in into cm

_____ cm

7 15.75 pt into litres

_____ litres

8 13.2 lb into kg

_____ kg

9 45 cm into ft

_____ ft

10 10 miles into km

_____ km

11 56 pints into litres

_____ litres

12 32 km into miles

_____ miles

Hit the target

Write these numbers on cards: one number on each.
Place all the cards face down. Each player takes 7 cards.

Decide on a target number, and a number to start from.
You may then look at your own cards.

Each player takes turns to play a card. The value is added to or subtracted from the starting number, following the instructions on the card.
The winner is the player who arrives at the target number.

Numbers for the cards:

+1	+2	+3	+4	+5	+6	+7	+8
−1	−2	−3	−4	−5	−6	−7	−8
+1	+2	+3	+4	+5	+6	+7	+8
−1	−2	−3	−4	−5	−6	−7	−8
+1	+2	+3	+4	+5	+6	+7	+8
−1	−2	−3	−4	−5	−6	−7	−8
+1	+2	+3	+4	+5	+6	+7	+8
−1	−2	−3	−4	−5	−6	−7	−8
+9	−9	+9	−9	+9	−9	+9	−9

14 Tables, graphs and charts

1   Venn diagrams

Venn diagrams are used
to sort information.

35, 40, 43, 45,
47, 55, 75.

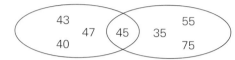

Numbers that   Numbers that
start with 4   end with 5

Exercise 14:1

Write the information in the spaces on the Venn diagrams.

1   18, 36, 44, 50, 51,
53, 54, 57, 60, 72.

Even numbers   Numbers that
start with 5

2   3, 4, 6, 8, 9, 12,
15, 16, 18, 20, 21.

Multiples   Multiples
of 3   of 4

3   41, 57, 59, 60, 61,
64, 66, 67, 75, 83.

Odd numbers   Numbers that
start with 6

4   List all the factors of 12:

_____

List all the factors of 16:

_____

Factors of 12   Factors of 16

2 Carroll diagrams

Carroll diagrams are used for sorting information in two different ways.

21, 22, 24, 25, 26, 27,
30, 31, 33, 36, 38

	Odd	Even
Numbers that have 3 tens	31 33	30 38 36
Numbers that have 2 tens	21 27 25	22 26 24

Exercise 14:2

In each question complete the Carroll diagram and answer the questions.

1 51, 72, 50, 59, 73, 71
52, 78, 76, 57, 75.

   a How many of these numbers are odd?

   b Which numbers have 5 tens and are also even?

	Odd	Even
Numbers that have 5 tens		
Numbers that have 7 tens		

2 70, 78, 43, 41, 75, 76
44, 72, 46, 47

   a Write down any numbers that have 7 tens and are odd.

   b How many of these numbers are even?

	Odd	Even
Numbers that have 7 tens		
Numbers that have 4 tens		

3 37, 55, 48, 24, 22, 53
33, 19, 88, 62, 11

   a How many numbers are there that have the same two digits?

   b Which numbers have different digits and are also odd?

	Odd	Even
Numbers that have 2 digits the same		
Numbers that have 2 digits that are different		

3 Frequency tables

Frequency tables are used to summarise information.

Exercise 14:3

Complete these frequency tables.

1 The shoe size worn by each pupil in a class.
4, 5, 3, 3, 6, 5, 4, 7, 4,
4, 7, 6, 5, 6, 7, 6, 8, 4,
3, 5, 5, 8, 6, 6, 4, 4, 6,
6, 5, 4
The tally for size 4 has been completed for you.

Shoe size	Tally	Frequency
3		
4	⊬⊬ |||	8
5		
6		
7		
8		
Total		

2 The registration group of the first forty pupils arriving at a school.
W, L, E, P, S, W, E, A, P,
E, S, W, W, W, S, L, L, E,
L, P, L, S, A, W, E, W, L,
S, P, S, P, L, A, S, E, A,
L, A, L, L

Registration group	Tally	Frequency
A		
E		
L		
P		
S		
W		
Total		

3 The number of fish caught by fishermen in a competition.
3, 2, 1, 4, 5, 5, 4, 5, 1,
6, 5, 5, 6, 4, 4, 3, 3, 3,
6, 3, 6, 2, 4, 4, 2, 3, 5,
2, 4, 6, 4, 6, 1, 4, 5, 3,
5, 5, 6, 4

Fish caught	Tally	Frequency
1		
2		
3		
4		
5		
6		
Total		

4 Bar charts

A bar chart is used to show information from a table.

Exercise 14:4

Complete these bar charts for the tables in Exercise 14:3.
One column in the first one is already drawn for you.

1

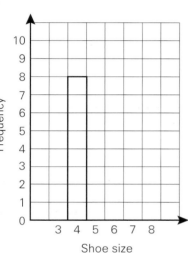

2

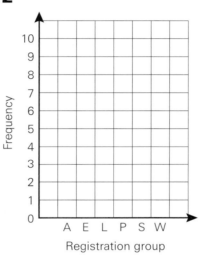

3

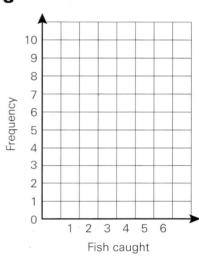

4 Draw the bar chart for this frequency table.
Make sure your graph is correctly labelled.

Pet	Frequency
Dogs	9
Cats	7
Fish	3
Mice	2
Other	5

5 Grouped frequency tables

When we have a lot of different information we put it in a grouped table to summarise it more easily.

Exercise 14:5

Complete these grouped frequency tables.

1 Number of deliveries made by a fleet of vans.

30 29 24 55 24 33 3
10 17 57 28 8 38 49
28 35 64 12 16 43 47
19 37 53 7 31 43 5
21 26 61 26 12 18 40

The tally for 10–19 deliveries has been completed for you.

Deliveries	Tally	Frequency
0–9		
10–19	⊬⊬ ||	7
20–29		
30–39		
40–49		
50–59		
60–69		

Total _____

2 Marks gained in a test.

43 32 12 14 20 32 38
63 55 7 22 57 43 14
33 65 29 35 22 18 4
51 28 59 44 27 11 31
48 35 46 8 49 25 37

Complete the class intervals for the marks.

Marks	Tally	Frequency
0–9		
10–19		

Total _____

3 Amounts spent in a shop.
£7.15, £26.12, £8.99, £31.54,
£48.55, £12.21, £45.53, £15.03,
£58.60, £34.25, £19.05, £36.22,
£37.05, £42.61, £17.83, £26.61,
£35.80, £41.63, £12.15, £53.84,
£27.41, £48.08, £24.89, £49.33,
£42.35, £30.27, £47.63, £14.88,
£43.65, £48.85, £16.41, £55.13,
£30.05, £28.82, £18.73.

Amount	Tally	Frequency
£0.00–£9.99		
£10.00–£19.99		

Total _____

6   Bar charts of grouped frequency tables

Exercise 14:6

Complete the bar charts for the tables in Exercise 14:5.
One column in the first one is already drawn for you.

1

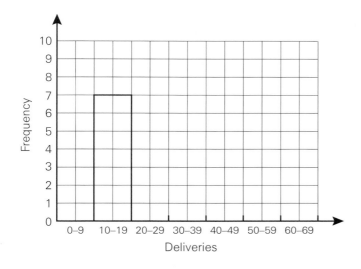

2

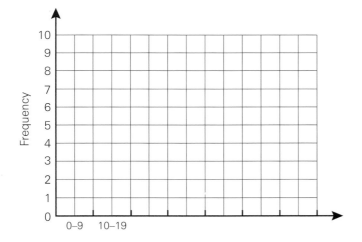

3

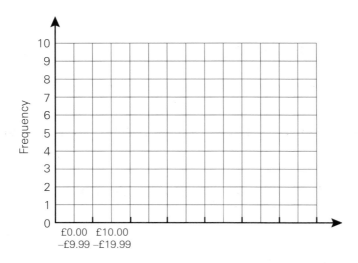

£0.00   £10.00
−£9.99 −£19.99

4   For these test marks

a complete the frequency table

b draw a bar chart

76 53 61 28 39 80 51 65
62 71 53 55 64 58 67 38
76 57 62 55 74 52 59 87
68 61 78 72 88 72 71 25
42 74 85 45 81 67 71 75

Marks	Tally	Frequency
21–30		
31–40		

Total _____

7 Pictograms

In a pictogram, symbols represent the information.

Exercise 14:7

1 The pictogram shows the number of cars passing a point in the road at 9 am each day for a week.

Monday	🚗 🚗 🚗
Tuesday	🚗 🚗 🚗 🚗
Wednesday	🚗 🚗 🚗
Thursday	
Friday	

Key: 🚗 = 10 cars

a How many cars were recorded on Monday?

_____

on Wednesday?

_____

b On which day were the most cars recorded?

_____

c On Thursday 15 cars passed, and on Friday 20 cars passed. Draw this information on the pictogram.

2 The pictogram shows the number of fish caught by five people in a competition.

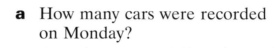

Usman	🐟 🐟 🐟
Tina	🐟 🐟 🐟 🐟
Hassan	🐟 🐟 🐟 🐟
Bill	
Roger	

Key: 🐟 = 4 fish

a How many fish did Usman catch?

_____

How many fish did Tina catch?

_____

b Who caught the fewest fish?

_____

c Bill caught 16 fish and Roger caught 14 fish. Add this information to the pictogram.

3   The pictogram shows the number of car parking tokens used over five days.

Monday	⊕ ⊕ ⊕ ⊕
Tuesday	⊕ ⊖
Wednesday	⊕ ⊕ ◖
Thursday	
Friday	

Key: ⊕ = 4 tokens

a How many tokens were needed on Monday?

_____

on Tuesday?

_____

b What is the total number of tokens needed on the first three days?

_____

c On Thursday 20 tokens were given out, and on Friday 9 tokens. Draw this information on the pictogram.

8   Using graphs and diagrams

Exercise 14:8

1   This is a bar-line graph of the number of times each score on a dice is thrown.

a Which score is thrown the most? _____

b Which score is thrown the least? _____

c Which two scores were thrown an equal number of times? _____

d How many times was a score **less than 4** thrown? _____

e How many times was the dice thrown? _____

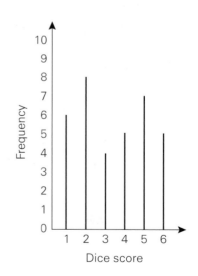

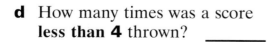

2 The graph shows the depth of water in a river mouth, read hourly.

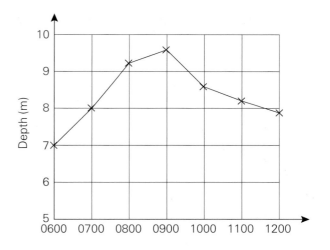

a What is the depth of water at 0800 hours? _____

b What is the depth of water at 1000 hours? _____

c At what time is the depth $9\frac{1}{2}$ metres? _____

d How far does the water rise between 0600 and 0800 hours? _____

3 The bar chart shows the number of vowels in a passage from a book.

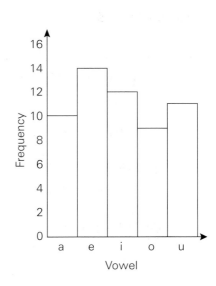

a Which vowel occurred the most? _____

b How many more were there of letter i than letter o? _____

c How many vowels were counted altogether? _____

4 The graph shows the number of flight departures for an airport.

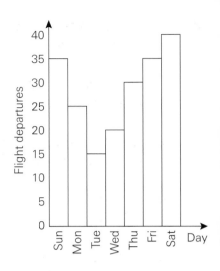

a How many departures were there on Thursday? _____

b On which day were there the least number of departures? _____

c On which day were there half as many departures as on Saturday? _____

d How many departures were there in total on the first three days of the week? _____

5 The bar chart shows the number of deliveries at a supermarket over six days.

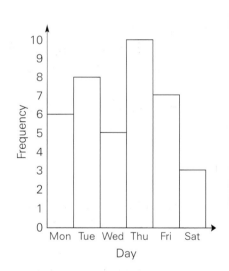

a On which day were there the most deliveries? _____

b On which day were there twice the number of deliveries as on Saturday? _____

c How many fewer deliveries were there on Wednesday than on Tuesday? _____

d Find the total number of deliveries for the week. _____

6 The graph shows the number of car sales at a showroom.

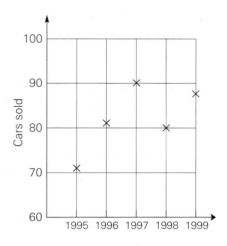

a How many cars were sold in 1996? _____

b During which year were the most cars sold? _____

c How many more cars were sold in 1997 compared to 1995? _____

d What is the total car sales for both 1998 and 1999? _____

9 Pie charts

A pie chart shows information about different categories.

Exercise 14:9

1 The results of a survey on favourite colours are shown in the pie chart.
There were 80 people in the survey.

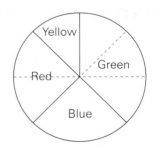

a Which was the most popular colour?

_____

b Which colours had the same popularity?

_____

c How many people preferred

i yellow: _____

ii green: _____

2 The pie chart shows the results
of a survey about pets.
40 people took part in the survey.

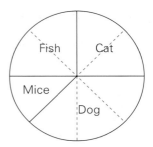

a Which was the least
popular pet?

_____

b Which pet was 3 times
as popular as mice?

_____

c How many people preferred

i cats? _____

ii dogs? _____

3 The pie chart shows the sales of
crisps at a school snack bar.

a Which flavour of crisp
is most popular?

_____

b Which flavour of crisp
is least popular?

_____

c Which flavour of crisp is
half as popular as
Cheese & Onion?

_____

1 Survey of pets

Conduct a survey to find out what kinds of household pets people keep.

Follow these instructions.

1 Ask other pupils and/or friends and relatives what pets they have. Keep a list of how many dogs, how many cats, etc., adding to your list of pets when necessary.
You might like to use a frequency table/tally table to keep a record as you ask about the pets.

2 Draw a neat frequency table, including tallies and totals for all pets.

3 Draw a bar chart and a pictogram to show your information.

4 Write a short explanation of what you have found. You could include details such as:

What is the most popular pet?

Which are the least popular pets?

Why do you think this is?

2 Fabfooty

For this game you need to make two special dice.

Copy these shapes onto card, cut them out, and make the dice. Colour them differently so you know which is which.

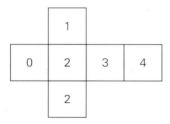

Dice H   Dice A

Dice H gives the Home team score, and dice A gives the Away team score.

If the dice are thrown together, do you think the result is more likely to be a Home win or an Away win?

Throw both the dice together, and write down the scores in the table.

Now throw them both again, to represent a second match. Enter the scores in the table.

Repeat this for more matches.

From your results, which team is more likely to win, the Home team, or the Away team?

Game number	H score	A score	Winner (H or A, or D for draw)
1			
2			
3			
4			
5			
6			
7			
8			
9			

The *Number Works!* homework resource is clearly linked to work presented in the *Number Works!* course book. Each chapter begins with a table which shows the link between each book, and which sections of the *Number Works!* book should be completed before each section of this *Number Works!* homework resource.

1 Number

This table shows how the sections in Chapter 1 in the *Number Works!* course book link to the sections in Chapter 1 of this homework book.

Course book section	2	3, 4	5, 6	7	8		9
Homework book section	1	2	3	4, 5, 6	7	8	9

EXERCISE 1:1

1	4735	**2**	7392	**3**	1743	**4**	8456
5	6884	**6**	5305	**7**	4550	**8**	3776

EXERCISE 1:2

1 Four thousand one hundred and thirty-seven
2 Three thousand five hundred and eighty-four
3 Eight thousand and sixty-one
4 Four thousand three hundred and seventy
5 Six thousand and sixty
6 Thirty-two thousand seven hundred and eighty
7 Ninety-seven thousand five hundred and forty-two
8 Six hundred and thirty thousand three hundred and eighty-one
9 One hundred and seventy-five thousand and sixty
10 Two hundred and thirty-four thousand and twenty-four
11 Three million, forty-two thousand, five hundred and ten
12 Twelve million, four hundred and three thousand, five hundred and nineteen

EXERCISE 1:3

1	2745	**2**	7604	**3**	4003
4	65 840	**5**	54 203	**6**	40 713
7	83 436	**8**	103 420	**9**	500 450
10	295 014	**11**	1 320 490	**12**	14 300 020

EXERCISE 1:4

1 3857, 2654, 2451, 1994
2 7100, 7033, 6900, 6804
3 4200, 4005, 3981, 3750
4 890, 848, 843, 821
5 18 851, 18 421, 17 453, 6547
6 65 217, 54 300, 51 207, 48 543
7 295, 426, 478, 486
8 274, 289, 300, 303
9 313, 422, 544, 622, 631
10 731, 750, 763, 787
11 99, 142, 268, 318, 581
12 5421, 5423, 5563, 5827

EXERCISE 1:5

1	=	**2**	>	**3**	<	**4**	<	**5**	>
6	<	**7**	=	**8**	>	**9**	=	**10**	>
11	=			**12**	<	**13**	1, 2, 3		
14	2, 4, 5, 6, 7, 9	**15**	6, 7, 9	**16**	7, 8, 9				
17	1, 2, 3, 4			**18**	6, 7, 9				

EXERCISE 1:6

1	>7	**2**	≤8	**3**	≤6	**4**	>3
5	<5	**6**	≥2	**7**	≥4	**8**	<7

9 0 1 2 3 4 5 6 7 8 9

10 0 1 2 3 4 5 6 7 8 9

11 0 1 2 3 4 5 6 7 8 9

12 0 1 2 3 4 5 6 7 8 9

13 0 1 2 3 4 5 6 7 8 9

14 0 1 2 3 4 5 6 7 8 9

15 0 1 2 3 4 5 6 7 8 9

16 0 1 2 3 4 5 6 7 8 9

EXERCISE 1:7

You should aim to be within 2 of each correct answer, since this is an estimate.

1	18	**2**	35	**3**	28	**4**	22	**5**	15
6	32	**7**	25	**8**	50	**9**	35		

EXERCISE 1:8

1	£7.50	**2**	£3.30	**3**	£18.70	**4**	£20.90
5	£87.10	**6**	£244.50	**7**	£8.40	**8**	£6.00
9	£4.70	**10**	£18.70	**11**	£9.20	**12**	£45.40
13	£54.20	**14**	£38.00					

EXERCISE 1:9

1	70	**2**	20	**3**	60	**4**	40	**5**	90
6	50	**7**	380	**8**	550	**9**	70	**10**	120
11	300	**12**	800	**13**	500	**14**	1000	**15**	900
16	600	**17**	2500	**18**	300	**19**	1400	**20**	700
21	5000	**22**	8000	**23**	1000	**24**	6000	**25**	7000

ACTIVITIES

1 **The disco**
Circled numbers:
55, 56, 57, 58, 59, 60, 61, 62, 63, 64, (allow 65)
Smallest number: 55
Largest number: 64 (allow 65)

2 **The numbers game**
Check your calculations using a calculator.
You may find it helpful to start each calculation with
the starting number.

2 Addition

This table shows how the sections in Chapter 2 in the
Number Works! course book link to the sections in
Chapter 2 of this homework book.

Course book section	2, 3	4, 5	6, 7	8, 9
Homework book section	1	2, 3	4	5

EXERCISE 2:1

1	77	**2**	77	**3**	179	**4**	93	**5**	498
6	92	**7**	548	**8**	999	**9**	84	**10**	999
11	109	**12**	990	**13**	2068	**14**	707	**15**	1171

These questions have carry numbers: 4, 6, 7, 9, 11, 12, 14, 15

EXERCISE 2:2

1	5121	**2**	444	**3**	1061	**4**	1745
5	1215	**6**	2213	**7**	5642	**8**	12 598
9	5030	**10**	11 161	**11**	9131	**12**	7304
13	5662	**14**	10 285	**15**	11 966		

EXERCISE 2:3

1	499	**2**	238	**3**	1346	**4**	1465
5	3092	**6**	1133	**7**	2392	**8**	1664
9	£2153	**10**	222				

EXERCISE 2:4

1	£3.67	**2**	£4.60	**3**	£10.34	**4**	£4.12
5	£11.80	**6**	£5.58	**7**	£6.55	**8**	£2.05
9	£14.30	**10**	£13.72	**11**	£2.99	**12**	£22.20
13	£14.98	**14**	£2.07	**15**	£9.20	**16**	£4.47

EXERCISE 2:5

1	24	**2**	25	**3**	23	**4**	24
5	26	**6**	28	**7**	27	**8**	32
9	33	**10**	26	**11**	36	**12**	27

EXERCISE 2:6

1	113	**2**	98	**3**	100	**4**	125	**5**	125
6	100	**7**	126	**8**	127	**9**	149	**10**	137
11	126	**12**	147	**13**	93	**14**	185	**15**	201

ACTIVITY

The numbers increase 3, 6, 10, 15, 23, . . .
The sum of the first 20 numbers is 210.
The totals of the even numbers are all even numbers them-
selves, and add up to 6, 12, 20, . . .
The totals of the odd numbers alternate between being an
odd, then an even number, and add up to 4, 9, 16, . . .
You can go as far as you wish with the adding up.

3 Subtraction

This table shows how the sections in Chapter 3 in the
Number Works! course book link to the sections in
Chapter 3 of this homework book.

Course book section	2	3	4, 5	6, 7	
Homework book section	1	2	3	4	5

EXERCISE 3:1

1	3–5, 5–6, 8–9, 1–8, 5–6								
2	12	**3**	35	**4**	44	**5**	23		
6	263	**7**	233	**8**	351	**9**	151		
10	313	**11**	451	**12**	243				

EXERCISE 3:2

1	19	**2**	28	**3**	36	**4**	46	**5**	18
6	26	**7**	15	**8**	19	**9**	29	**10**	25
11	36	**12**	46	**13**	27	**14**	37	**15**	28

EXERCISE 3:3

1	4809	**2**	3878	**3**	885	**4**	4229	**5**	1807
6	545	**7**	599	**8**	662	**9**	7687	**10**	8642
11	1416	**12**	3847	**13**	889	**14**	2268	**15**	769

EXERCISE 3:4

1	159	**2**	338	**3**	4878	**4**	4694	**5**	1387
6	5763	**7**	4666	**8**	4536	**9**	3656	**10**	4272
11	3666	**12**	2747	**13**	1459	**14**	6485	**15**	1993

EXERCISE 3:5

1	£4.35	**2**	824	**3**	625	**4**	58	**5**	952
6	27	**7**	1642	**8**	1010 g	**9**	24 310	**10**	57

ACTIVITIES

1 Darts and numbers

You need to understand the way that a dartboard is put together. The outer circle trebles numbers, and the inner circle doubles numbers. Try to maximise your score by throwing darts into the sectors with the larger numbers. The largest number that you can score with three darts is 180.

2 Numbers

A game of strategy based on darts scoring.

4 Times tables

This table shows how the sections in Chapter 4 in the *Number Works!* course book link to the sections in Chapter 4 of this homework book.

Course book section	2	3	4	5	6
Homework book section	1	2	3	4	5

EXERCISE 4:1

1	6	**2**	10	**3**	12	**4**	15	**5**	90
6	30	**7**	18	**8**	70	**9**	30	**10**	8
11	50	**12**	45	**13**	40p	**14**	20	**15**	14
16	25	**17**	60	**18**	100				

EXERCISE 4:2

1	10	**2**	32	**3**	35	**4**	16	**5**	40
6	18	**7**	20	**8**	24	**9**	60	**10**	36
11	25	**12**	30	**13**	20	**14**	28	**15**	50
16	21	**17**	40	**18**	16				

EXERCISE 4:3

1	12	**2**	8	**3**	42	**4**	20	**5**	64
6	35	**7**	27	**8**	48	**9**	24	**10**	90
11	49	**12**	72	**13**	54	**14**	24	**15**	63
16	16	**17**	35	**18**	56				

EXERCISE 4:4

1	9	**2**	9	**3**	8	**4**	7	**5**	9
6	9	**7**	8	**8**	7	**9**	6	**10**	8
11	7	**12**	10	**13**	6	**14**	6	**15**	7
16	8	**17**	9	**18**	8 g				

EXERCISE 4:5

1	11	**2**	9	**3**	6	**4**	8	**5**	7
6	7	**7**	6	**8**	9	**9**	7	**10**	8
11	7	**12**	9	**13**	9	**14**	8 m	**15**	6
16	9	**17**	4	**18**	8				

ACTIVITY

Tables bingo

Prepare your questions well in advance of the game. You will also need several questions for each number if you wish to play more than one game.

5 Multiplication

This table shows how the sections in Chapter 5 in the *Number Works!* course book link to the sections in Chapter 5 of this homework book.

Course book section	2, 3	4	5, 6	7	8
Homework book section	1	2	3	4	5

EXERCISE 5:1

1	492	**2**	1025	**3**	408	**4**	3234
5	3228	**6**	12 624	**7**	12 384	**8**	2525
9	5076	**10**	12 036	**11**	7090	**12**	7143

EXERCISE 5:2

1	4375	**2**	5648	**3**	2292	**4**	3330
5	5805	**6**	2912	**7**	1008	**8**	1575
9	9744	**10**	20 296	**11**	14 652	**12**	10 878
13	8396	**14**	21 168	**15**	37 758	**16**	43 857
17	27 160	**18**	66 968	**19**	17 142	**20**	45 353

EXERCISE 5:3

1	2740	**2**	632 000	**3**	5600	**4**	60 000
5	31 090	**6**	15 600	**7**	2260	**8**	44 100
9	150 500	**10**	200 000	**11**	30 320	**12**	175 000
13	218 000	**14**	31 500	**15**	4 026 000	**16**	739 800

EXERCISE 5:4

1	444	**2**	1768	**3**	1476	**4**	600
5	2116	**6**	767	**7**	792	**8**	1792
9	5928	**10**	8051	**11**	1092	**12**	4788

EXERCISE 5:5

1	9683	**2**	6528	**3**	3888	**4**	14 560
5	8343	**6**	24 434	**7**	29 438	**8**	49 042
9	19 635	**10**	24 975	**11**	45 441	**12**	12 814
13	22 506	**14**	160 332	**15**	172 557	**16**	256 239

ACTIVITY

When you multiply the unit numbers of the two numbers, you get the unit number of the answer.

Problem	Units answer
72×43	$2 \times 3 = 6$
93×112	$3 \times 2 = 6$
12×63	$2 \times 3 = 6$
730×49	$0 \times 9 = 0$

In the second table, multiply any two numbers that end in 2 and 3, or any two numbers that end in 6 and 1.

6 Division

This table shows how the sections in Chapter 6 in the *Number Works!* course book link to the sections in Chapter 6 of this homework book.

Course book section	2, 3	4	5, 6	7	8
Homework book section	1	2	3	4	5, 6

EXERCISE 6:1

1	45r2	**2**	133r1	**3**	138r2	**4**	2668r1
5	123r3	**6**	45r2	**7**	87r7	**8**	2967r2
9	1240r5	**10**	1130r5	**11**	743r2	**12**	468r2

EXERCISE 6:2

1	12.25	**2**	104.5	**3**	397.5	**4**	15.125
5	784.5	**6**	435.75	**7**	22.625	**8**	443.5
9	1394.5	**10**	376.5	**11**	127.375	**12**	415.75

EXERCISE 6:3

1	3	**2**	5	**3**	2	**4**	70
5	80	**6**	90	**7**	4	**8**	3
9	30	**10**	40	**11**	5	**12**	3
13	50	**14**	5000	**15**	20	**16**	200

EXERCISE 6:4

1	1320	**2**	145	**3**	241	**4**	233
5	342	**6**	4040	**7**	465	**8**	783
9	874	**10**	708	**11**	352	**12**	897

EXERCISE 6:5

1	7	**2**	10	**3**	4	**4**	9 weeks
5	16p	**6**	9	**7**	11	**8**	8
9	13	**10**	12				

EXERCISE 6:6

1	45	**2**	9	**3**	783	**4**	1136	**5**	8
6	£9683	**7**	£542	**8**	621 g	**9**	947	**10**	3924

ACTIVITIES

Divisions of 100

a 2, 4, 10, 20, 50

b $100 \div 2 = 50$; $100 \div 4 = 25$;
  $100 \div 6 = 16.666\ldots$; $100 \div 8 = 12.5$
  $100 \div 10 = 10$; $100 \div 12 = 8.333\ldots$;
  $100 \div 14 = 7.142857142857\ldots$
  $100 \div 16 = 6.25$; $100 \div 18 = 5.555\ldots$
  If the numbers do not divide so that they give a decimal answer that has a number of decimal places, then the decimal does recur and have a pattern.

c 1, 5, 25.

d $100 \div 3 = 33.333\ldots$; $100 \div 5 = 20$;
  $100 \div 7 = 14.2857142857\ldots$
  $100 \div 9 = 11.111..$; $100 \div 11 = 9.090909\ldots$;
  $100 \div 13 = 7.6923076923\ldots$; $100 \div 15 = 6.666\ldots$;
  $100 \div 17 = 5.882352941$; $100 \div 19 = 5.263157895$
  Most of the numbers do have a repeating pattern.

e Numbers that are multiples of three, and prime numbers, amongst others.

7 Decimals

This table shows how the sections in Chapter 7 in the *Number Works!* course book link to the sections in Chapter 7 of this homework book.

Course book section	2	3	4	5	6	7	8	9
Homework book section	1	2	3	4	5	6, 7	8	9

EXERCISE 7:1

DECIMAL	H	T	U	•	t	h	th	FRACTION
0.7			0	•	7			$\frac{7}{10}$
0.67			0	•	6	7		$\frac{67}{100}$
0.08			0	•	0	8		$\frac{8}{100}$
2.37			2	•	3	7		$2\frac{37}{100}$
1.004			1	•	0	0	4	$1\frac{4}{1000}$

FRACTION	H	T	U	•	t	h	th	DECIMAL
$\frac{3}{100}$			0	•	0	3		0.03
$2\frac{7}{10}$			2	•	7			2.7
$\frac{11}{1000}$			0	•	0	1	1	0.011
$4\frac{3}{100}$			4	•	0	3		4.03
$3\frac{9}{10}$			3	•	9			3.9

EXERCISE 7:2

1 6.7 cm	**2** 3.2 amps	**3** 1.7 kg	**4** 0.6 g
5 6.2 mm	**6** 4.4	**7** 7.3 m	**8** 34 mph
9 1.3 °C	**10** 5.3 litres		

EXERCISE 7:3

1 2.02, 2.0, 0.220, 0.022
2 8.0, 0.8, 0.08, 0.008
3 2.1, 1.2, 0.21, 0.12
4 0.574, 0.572, 0.565, 0.556
5 9.99, 9.904, 9.9, 9.804
6 7.306, 7.305, 7.204, 7.202
7 8.701, 8.8, 8.801, 8.88
8 0.125, 0.525, 0.55, 1.25
9 4.022, 4.202, 4.222
10 1.08, 9.08, 9.8, 10.8
11 0.0206, 0.0266, 0.06606
12 3.033, 3.303, 3.33

EXERCISE 7:4

1 7.76	**2** 13.07	**3** 10.47	**4** 10.43
5 16.11	**6** 23.001	**7** 6.605	**8** 22.32
9 10	**10** 3.196	**11** 12.006	**12** 14.225

EXERCISE 7:5

1 4.093	**2** 3.62	**3** 0.977	**4** 2.099
5 0.39	**6** 0.977	**7** 0.09	**8** 0.111
9 0.317	**10** 0.036	**11** 0.118	**12** 0.938

EXERCISE 7:6

1 70.2	**2** 58.95	**3** 49.08	**4** 17.04
5 12.104	**6** 56.48	**7** 248.2	**8** 39.2
9 35.65	**10** 37.92	**11** 66.65	**12** 97.24

EXERCISE 7:7

1 0.26	**2** 12.48	**3** 2.94	**4** 23.45
5 1.08	**6** 0.64	**7** 77.66	**8** 2.205
9 55.25	**10** 0.2992	**11** 67.58	**12** 16.548

EXERCISE 7:8

1 25.4	**2** 104.2	**3** 0.013	**4** 0.0175
5 5.5	**6** 0.1042	**7** 70.5	**8** 5.1
9 60	**10** 0.54	**11** 0.012	**12** 991.4

EXERCISE 7:9

1 13.42	**2** 2.43	**3** 14.51	**4** 2.1435
5 0.1573	**6** 23.625	**7** 47.34	**8** 5.6072
9 1.0435	**10** 26.514	**11** 9.4755	**12** 49.04

ACTIVITY

Number parts

Section A:

The maximum product of the 2 parts for any number is found by dividing that number exactly into 2 parts:

maximum for 6 is $3 \times 3 = 9$;

maximum for 7 is $3.5 \times 3.5 = 12.25$;

maximum for 8 is $4 \times 4 = 16$, etc.

The rule for finding the maximum for any number is therefore:

$n/2 \times n/2$ where n is the number.

Section B:

The maximum product of the 3 parts for any number is found by dividing that number exactly into 3 parts. Using a calculator you may get some very long decimals when you divide by 3.

maximum for 5 is $1.666 \times 1.666 \times 1.666$
$= 4.63$ (rounded)

maximum for 6 is $2 \times 2 \times 2 = 8$

maximum for 7 is $2.333 \times 2.333 \times 2.333$
$= 12.7$ (rounded)

The rule for finding the maximum for any number is therefore:

$n/3 \times n/3 \times n/3$ where n is the number.

Section C:

The maximum product of the 4 parts for any number is found by dividing that number exactly into 4 parts. The rule for finding the maximum for any number is:
$n/4 \times n/4 \times n/4 \times n/4$.

8   Number properties and sequences

This table shows how the sections in Chapter 8 in the *Number Works!* course book link to the sections in Chapter 8 of this homework book.

Course book section	2	3	4	5	6	7, 8
Homework book section	1	2	3	4	5	6

EXERCISE 8:1

1 3, 9, 13, 15 **2** 2, 8, 20 **3** 15, 20
4 3, 9, 15 **5** 2, 3 **6** 3, 5, 25
7 6, 12, 30, 40 **8** 5, 25, 30, 40 **9** 12, 40
10 3, 5 **11** 1, 2, 3, 6, 7, 14, 21, 42
12 1, 2, 4, 8, 16 **13** 1, 2, 4, 5, 10, 20
14 1, 3, 5, 15 **15** 1, 3, 7, 21
16 1, 2, 3, 4, 6, 8, 12, 24

EXERCISE 8:2

1 6, 12, 18 **2** 12, 24, 36 **3** 12, 24, 36
4 10, 20, 30 **5** 30 **6** 6
7 12 **8** 18 **9** 1, 2, 3, 6
10 1, 3 **11** 1, 2, 4, 5, 10, 20 **12** 1, 7
13 9 **14** 16 **15** 10
16 7

EXERCISE 8:3

1 2, 3, 5, 7, 11, 13, 17, 19, 23, 29
2 1, 4, 9, 16, 25, 36, 49, 64, 81, 100
3 1, 3, 6, 10, 15, 21, 28, 36, 45, 55
4 2, 13; 5, 11; 5, 19; 23, 29, 41
5 4, 64; 16, 49, 100; 9, 36; 25, 64, 81.
6 **a** 2, 3 **b** 2, 3 **c** 2, 3 **d** 2, 3, 5
7 **a** 25 **b** 64 **c** 36 **d** 1

EXERCISE 8:4

1

Diagram	1	2	3	4	5
Number of squares	2	4	6	8	10

2

Diagram	1	2	3	4	5
Number of sticks	3	6	9	12	15

3

Diagram	1	2	3	4	5
Number of dots	5	8	11	14	17

4

Diagram	1	2	3	4	5
Number of sticks	4	7	10	13	16

5

Diagram	1	2	3	4	5
Distance around perimeter	6	8	10	12	14

6

Diagram	1	2	3	4	5
Number of sticks	3	5	7	9	11

EXERCISE 8:5

1 20, 31, 42, 53, 64 **2** 31, 27, 23, 19, 15, 11
3 3, 5, 8, 12, 17, 23 **4** 10, 13, 18, 25, 34, 45
5 15, 16, 21, 30, 43, 60 **6** 9, 14, 19, 24, 29, 34
7 17, 23, 29, 35, 41, 47 **8** 17, 20, 23, 26, 29, 32
9 16, 25, 34, 43, 52, 61 **10** 9, 16, 23, 30, 37, 44
11 20, 17, 14, 11, 8, 5 **12** 17, 20, 23, 26, 29, 32

EXERCISE 8:6

1

Term number	1	2	3	4	5	6
Term	3	5	7	9	11	13

Rule: $\times 2 + 1$

2

Term number	1	2	3	4	5	6
Term	5	7	9	11	13	15

Rule: $\times 2 + 3$

3

Term number	1	2	3	4	5	6
Term	5	8	11	14	17	20

Rule: × 3 + 2

4

Term number	1	2	3	4	5	6
Term	5	9	13	17	21	25

Rule: × 4 + 1

5

Term number	1	2	3	4	5	6
Term	1	3	5	7	9	11

Rule: × 2 − 1

6

Term number	1	2	3	4	5	6
Term	1	4	7	10	13	16

Rule: × 3 − 2

7

Term number	1	2	3	4	5	6
Term	3	7	11	15	19	23

Rule: × 4 − 1

8

Term number	1	2	3	4	5	6
Term	7	12	17	22	27	32

Rule: × 5 + 2

ACTIVITIES

1 Prime number display
Prime numbers: 2, 3, 5, 7, 11, 13, 17, 19, 23, 29, 31, 37, 41, 43, 47, 53, 59, 61, 67, 71, 73, 79, 83, 89, 97

2 Dots and lines

Dots	1	2	3	4	5	6
Lines	0	1	3	6	10	15

a 45   **b** 105   **c** 190

The pattern of numbers is the triangle numbers.
The rule is
dots × (dots −1) ÷ 2

9   Fractions – addition and subtraction

This table shows how the sections in Chapter 9 in the *Number Works!* course book link to the sections in Chapter 9 of this homework book.

Course book section	2	3, 4	5	6	7	8
Homework book section	1	2	3	4	5	6

EXERCISE 9:1

1 $\frac{1}{3}$ **2** $\frac{3}{5}$ **3** $\frac{2}{3}$ **4** $\frac{5}{6}$

5 $\frac{5}{8}$ **6** $\frac{3}{7}$

7 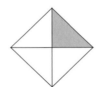   **8**

9 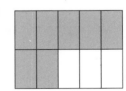   **10**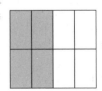

11   **12**

EXERCISE 9:2

1 $\dfrac{2}{3} = \dfrac{4}{6} = \dfrac{6}{9} = \dfrac{8}{12}$ **2** $\dfrac{4}{6} = \dfrac{8}{12} = \dfrac{12}{18} = \dfrac{16}{24}$

3 $\dfrac{3}{5} = \dfrac{6}{10} = \dfrac{9}{15} = \dfrac{12}{20}$ **4** $\dfrac{3}{4} = \dfrac{6}{8} = \dfrac{9}{12} = \dfrac{12}{16}$

5 $\dfrac{3}{4} = \dfrac{9}{12}$ **6** $\dfrac{1}{3} = \dfrac{5}{15}$ **7** $\dfrac{2}{3} = \dfrac{6}{9}$ **8** $\dfrac{3}{4} = \dfrac{15}{20}$

9 $\dfrac{4}{5} = \dfrac{8}{10}$ **10** $\dfrac{4}{5} = \dfrac{12}{15}$ **11** $\dfrac{5}{6} = \dfrac{35}{42}$ **12** $\dfrac{2}{3} = \dfrac{8}{12}$

EXERCISE 9:3

1 $\dfrac{4}{5}, \dfrac{2}{3}$ **2** $\dfrac{2}{5}, \dfrac{3}{8}$ **3** $\dfrac{4}{9}, \dfrac{2}{7}$

4 $\dfrac{3}{10}, \dfrac{2}{7}$ **5** $\dfrac{7}{8}, \dfrac{3}{6}$ **6** $\dfrac{2}{3}, \dfrac{3}{5}$

7 $\dfrac{5}{8}, \dfrac{2}{3}$ **8** $\dfrac{2}{3}, \dfrac{7}{10}$ **9** $\dfrac{3}{5}, \dfrac{5}{7}$

10 $\dfrac{8}{10}, \dfrac{7}{8}$ **11** $\dfrac{7}{9}, \dfrac{4}{5}$ **12** $\dfrac{5}{9}, \dfrac{3}{5}$

EXERCISE 9:4

1 $\dfrac{3}{4}$ **2** $\dfrac{2}{7}$ **3** $\dfrac{3}{4}$ **4** $\dfrac{2}{3}$ **5** $\dfrac{1}{4}$

6 $\dfrac{3}{5}$ **7** $\dfrac{1}{3}$ **8** $\dfrac{4}{9}$ **9** $\dfrac{5}{6}$ **10** $\dfrac{3}{5}$

11 $\dfrac{5}{7}$ **12** $\dfrac{3}{4}$ **13** $\dfrac{9}{20}$ **14** $\dfrac{2}{5}$ **15** $\dfrac{3}{4}$

16 $\dfrac{3}{5}$

EXERCISE 9:5

1 $\dfrac{4}{5}$ **2** $\dfrac{5}{6}$ **3** $\dfrac{7}{9}$ **4** $\dfrac{5}{8}$ **5** $\dfrac{4}{5}$

6 $\dfrac{3}{4}$ **7** $\dfrac{5}{8}$ **8** $\dfrac{9}{32}$ **9** $\dfrac{11}{16}$ **10** $\dfrac{21}{32}$

11 $\dfrac{11}{32}$ **12** $\dfrac{11}{16}$

EXERCISE 9:6

1 $\dfrac{1}{6}$ **2** $\dfrac{2}{7}$ **3** $\dfrac{5}{12}$ **4** $\dfrac{3}{10}$ **5** $\dfrac{5}{8}$

6 $\dfrac{1}{8}$ **7** $\dfrac{11}{16}$ **8** $\dfrac{3}{16}$ **9** $\dfrac{1}{16}$ **10** $\dfrac{9}{16}$

11 $\dfrac{1}{16}$ **12** $\dfrac{17}{32}$

ACTIVITY

Equivalence poster

$\frac{1}{2}$	$\frac{2}{4}$	$\frac{3}{6}$	$\frac{4}{8}$	$\frac{5}{10}$	$\frac{6}{12}$	$\frac{7}{14}$	$\frac{8}{16}$	$\frac{9}{18}$	$\frac{10}{20}$
$\frac{1}{3}$	$\frac{2}{6}$	$\frac{3}{9}$	$\frac{4}{12}$	$\frac{5}{15}$	$\frac{6}{18}$	$\frac{7}{21}$	$\frac{8}{24}$	$\frac{9}{27}$	$\frac{10}{30}$
$\frac{1}{4}$	$\frac{2}{8}$	$\frac{3}{12}$	$\frac{4}{16}$	$\frac{5}{20}$	$\frac{6}{24}$	$\frac{7}{28}$	$\frac{8}{32}$	$\frac{9}{36}$	$\frac{10}{40}$
$\frac{1}{5}$	$\frac{2}{10}$	$\frac{3}{15}$	$\frac{4}{20}$	$\frac{5}{25}$	$\frac{6}{30}$	$\frac{7}{35}$	$\frac{8}{40}$	$\frac{9}{45}$	$\frac{10}{50}$
$\frac{1}{6}$	$\frac{2}{12}$	$\frac{3}{18}$	$\frac{4}{24}$	$\frac{5}{30}$	$\frac{6}{36}$	$\frac{7}{42}$	$\frac{8}{48}$	$\frac{9}{54}$	$\frac{10}{60}$
$\frac{1}{7}$	$\frac{2}{14}$	$\frac{3}{21}$	$\frac{4}{28}$	$\frac{5}{35}$	$\frac{6}{42}$	$\frac{7}{49}$	$\frac{8}{56}$	$\frac{9}{63}$	$\frac{10}{70}$
$\frac{1}{8}$	$\frac{2}{16}$	$\frac{3}{24}$	$\frac{4}{32}$	$\frac{5}{40}$	$\frac{6}{48}$	$\frac{7}{56}$	$\frac{8}{64}$	$\frac{9}{72}$	$\frac{10}{80}$
$\frac{1}{9}$	$\frac{2}{18}$	$\frac{3}{27}$	$\frac{4}{36}$	$\frac{5}{45}$	$\frac{6}{54}$	$\frac{7}{63}$	$\frac{8}{72}$	$\frac{9}{81}$	$\frac{10}{90}$
$\frac{1}{10}$	$\frac{2}{20}$	$\frac{3}{30}$	$\frac{4}{40}$	$\frac{5}{50}$	$\frac{6}{60}$	$\frac{7}{70}$	$\frac{8}{80}$	$\frac{9}{90}$	$\frac{10}{100}$
$\frac{1}{11}$	$\frac{2}{22}$	$\frac{3}{33}$	$\frac{4}{44}$	$\frac{5}{55}$	$\frac{6}{66}$	$\frac{7}{77}$	$\frac{8}{88}$	$\frac{9}{99}$	$\frac{10}{110}$
$\frac{1}{12}$	$\frac{2}{24}$	$\frac{3}{36}$	$\frac{4}{48}$	$\frac{5}{60}$	$\frac{6}{72}$	$\frac{7}{84}$	$\frac{8}{96}$	$\frac{9}{108}$	$\frac{10}{120}$
$\frac{1}{13}$	$\frac{2}{26}$	$\frac{3}{39}$	$\frac{4}{52}$	$\frac{5}{65}$	$\frac{6}{78}$	$\frac{7}{91}$	$\frac{8}{104}$	$\frac{9}{117}$	$\frac{10}{130}$
$\frac{1}{14}$	$\frac{2}{28}$	$\frac{3}{42}$	$\frac{4}{56}$	$\frac{5}{70}$	$\frac{6}{84}$	$\frac{7}{98}$	$\frac{8}{112}$	$\frac{9}{126}$	$\frac{10}{140}$
$\frac{1}{15}$	$\frac{2}{30}$	$\frac{3}{45}$	$\frac{4}{60}$	$\frac{5}{75}$	$\frac{6}{90}$	$\frac{7}{105}$	$\frac{8}{120}$	$\frac{9}{135}$	$\frac{10}{150}$
$\frac{1}{16}$	$\frac{2}{32}$	$\frac{3}{48}$	$\frac{4}{64}$	$\frac{5}{80}$	$\frac{6}{96}$	$\frac{7}{112}$	$\frac{8}{128}$	$\frac{9}{144}$	$\frac{10}{160}$

10 Fractions – multiplication and division

This table shows how the sections in Chapter 10 in the *Number Works!* course book link to the sections in Chapter 10 of this homework book.

Course book section	2	3	4	5	6	7	8
Homework book section	1	2	3	4	5	6	7

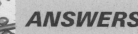

EXERCISE 10:1

1 $\frac{7}{2}$ **2** $\frac{22}{5}$ **3** $\frac{8}{3}$ **4** $\frac{31}{4}$ **5** $\frac{37}{10}$

6 $\frac{17}{6}$ **7** $\frac{15}{4}$ **8** $\frac{29}{3}$ **9** $\frac{23}{5}$ **10** $\frac{23}{9}$

11 $\frac{55}{10}$ **12** $\frac{20}{3}$ **13** $\frac{13}{10}$ **14** $\frac{41}{7}$

15 $\frac{77}{9}$ **16** $\frac{29}{5}$

EXERCISE 10:2

1 $3\frac{1}{2}$ **2** $2\frac{1}{4}$ **3** $3\frac{1}{3}$ **4** $2\frac{2}{9}$

5 $7\frac{1}{3}$ **6** $1\frac{1}{8}$ **7** $4\frac{4}{7}$ **8** $7\frac{1}{6}$

9 $8\frac{4}{5}$ **10** $6\frac{3}{10}$ **11** $3\frac{7}{12}$ **12** $8\frac{7}{8}$

13 $6\frac{8}{9}$ **14** $4\frac{7}{10}$ **15** $7\frac{5}{8}$ **16** $8\frac{1}{4}$

17 $3\frac{7}{10}$ **18** $4\frac{5}{9}$ **19** $4\frac{5}{12}$ **20** $9\frac{4}{5}$

EXERCISE 10:3

1 $2\frac{4}{10}, 2\frac{3}{8}$ **2** $5\frac{4}{5}, 5\frac{5}{7}$

3 $4\frac{3}{4}, 4\frac{2}{5}$ **4** $3\frac{9}{10}, 3\frac{7}{9}$

5 $6\frac{1}{2}, 6\frac{2}{7}$ **6** $5\frac{5}{7}, 5\frac{8}{12}$

7 $2\frac{2}{3}, 3\frac{4}{5}, 3\frac{7}{8}$ **8** $4\frac{1}{3}, 5\frac{3}{10}, 5\frac{2}{5}$

9 $3\frac{5}{7}, 3\frac{4}{5}, 4\frac{1}{3}$ **10** $4\frac{3}{5}, 6\frac{4}{7}, 6\frac{7}{9}$

EXERCISE 10:4

1 £1.32   **2** 221 km   **3** 321   **4** £49.60
5 17 kg   **6** 106.5 mm   **7** 1530   **8** 7.38 m
9 16.8 kg   **10** £6.15   **11** 405   **12** £3765

EXERCISE 10:5

1 $\frac{1}{4}$ **2** $\frac{1}{5}$ **3** $\frac{7}{10}$ **4** $\frac{5}{16}$ **5** $\frac{23}{63}$

6 $\frac{2}{7}$ **7** $\frac{4}{11}$ **8** $\frac{5}{9}$ **9** $\frac{7}{12}$ **10** $\frac{63}{365}$

EXERCISE 10:6

1 $\frac{8}{15}$ **2** $\frac{25}{42}$ **3** $\frac{2}{7}$ **4** 8

5 $1\frac{1}{7}$ **6** $\frac{2}{3}$ **7** $12\frac{1}{2}$ **8** $\frac{11}{20}$

EXERCISE 10:7

1 $\frac{3}{4}$ **2** $\frac{1}{4}$ **3** $\frac{9}{16}$ **4** $\frac{4}{45}$

5 $1\frac{3}{7}$ **6** $\frac{7}{30}$ **7** $2\frac{1}{2}$ **8** $1\frac{1}{2}$

ACTIVITIES

1 Fraction divisions

The answer to all these problems is 1.
The reason is that anything divided by itself is always 1.
($2 \div 2 = 1$, $3 \div 3 = 1$, etc. for whole numbers. The same applies to fractions.)

2 Fractions of £1

a $\frac{1}{3}$ of £1 is 33.3333 . . . p

b $\frac{1}{4}$ of £1 is 25p

c $\frac{1}{6}$ of £1 is 16.6666 . . . p

The answers tell you that it is not always possible to find the exact fraction of £1.
Dividing £1 by the following numbers gives you a whole number:
2, 4, 5, 10, 20, 25, 50.

3 Fractions of a circle

a

Fraction	$\frac{1}{2}$	$\frac{1}{3}$	$\frac{1}{4}$	$\frac{1}{5}$	$\frac{1}{6}$	$\frac{1}{7}$	$\frac{1}{8}$	$\frac{1}{9}$	$\frac{1}{10}$
Angle	180°	120°	90°	72°	60°	51°	45°	40°	36°

Note that $\frac{1}{7}$ of 360° is not an exact answer: it is 51.4° rounded to one decimal place.

b $\frac{1}{12}, \frac{1}{15}, \frac{1}{18}, \frac{1}{20}, \frac{1}{24}, \frac{1}{30}, \frac{1}{36}, \frac{1}{40}, \frac{1}{45}, \frac{1}{60}, \frac{1}{72}, \frac{1}{90}, \frac{1}{120}, \frac{1}{180}$

c

$\frac{1}{2}$ 180° $\frac{1}{3}$ 120° $\frac{1}{4}$ 90° $\frac{1}{5}$ 72° $\frac{1}{6}$ 60°

$\frac{1}{7}$ 51.4° $\frac{1}{8}$ 45° $\frac{1}{9}$ 40° $\frac{1}{10}$ 36°

11 Ratios

This table shows how the sections in Chapter 11 in the *Number Works!* course book link to the sections in Chapter 11 of the homework book.

Course book section	2, 3	4	5	6	7	8
Homework book section	1	2	3	4	5	6

EXERCISE 11:1

1 3 : 4	**2** 6 : 1	**3** 1 : 4	**4** 2 : 1
5 1 : 3	**6** 1 : 5	**7** 1 : 10	**8** 1 : 20
9 3 : 8	**10** 2 : 7	**11** 1 : 5	**12** 1 : 4
13 1 : 6	**14** 1 : 4	**15** 4 : 15	

EXERCISE 11:2

1 14p	**2** 33	**3** 14 litres	**4** 15 km
5 £4.50	**6** 3.2 m	**7** 122 g	**8** 40 m

EXERCISE 11:3

1 63p	**2** £108	**3** 143 km
4 22.5 kg	**5** £4.80	**6** 69 min
7 192 g	**8** 765 miles	

EXERCISE 11:4

1 14	**2** 9 cm	**3** 3 days	**4** 16 min
5 20 days	**6** 15 days	**7** 1½ h	**8** 80 min

EXERCISE 11:5

1

haricot beans	525 g
onions	3
bacon	150 g
chicken drumsticks	6
stock	1350 ml

2

self-raising flour	625 g
margarine	375 g
demerera sugar	200 g
mixed dried fruit	375 g
milk	5
eggs	5

3 42   **4** 18   **5** 30   **6** 18

EXERCISE 11:6

1 £4.96, £7.44	**2** 9.3 litres, 15.5 litres
3 13.68 m, 17.1 m	**4** 14.25 kg, 23.75 kg
5 12 boys, 16 girls	**6** £1.30, £5.20
7 270	**8** 68

ACTIVITIES

1 Recipes
You could present the new recipes as a cookbook of your own.

2 Mixing concrete

Foundations

Cement	1	2	3	5	8	10	12	20
Sand	2	4	6	10	16	20	24	40
Stone	4	8	12	20	32	40	48	80

Paths

Cement	1	2	4	5	8	11	16	20
Sand	2	4	8	10	16	22	32	40
Stone	3	6	12	15	24	33	48	60

12 Percentages

This table shows how the sections in Chapter 12 in the *Number Works!* course book link to the sections in Chapter 12 of this homework book.

Course book section	2	3	4	5	6	7	8	9
Homework book section	1, 2	3	4	5	6	7	8	9

EXERCISE 12:1

1 20%   **2** 45%   **3** 73%   **4** 88%

5

6

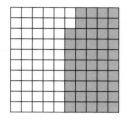 
7 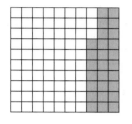 **8**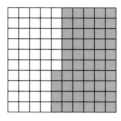

9 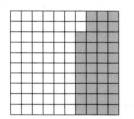 **10**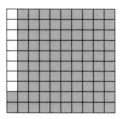

11 **12**

EXERCISE 12:2

As these are only estimates your answer may be 2% more or less than the value given here.

1	20%	**2**	80%	**3**	60%	**4**	30%
5	65%	**6**	12%	**7**	77%	**8**	43%

9   **10**   **11**

12   **13**   **14**

15   **16**

EXERCISE 12:3

Percent-age	Frac-tion	Decimal	Percent-age	Frac-age	Decimal tion
3%	$\frac{3}{100}$	0.03	32%	$\frac{32}{100}$ $\frac{8}{25}$	0.32
16%	$\frac{16}{100}$ $\frac{4}{25}$	0.16	41%	$\frac{41}{100}$	0.41
77%	$\frac{77}{100}$	0.77	68%	$\frac{68}{100}$ $\frac{17}{25}$	0.68
80%	$\frac{80}{100}$ $\frac{4}{5}$	0.8	20%	$\frac{20}{100}$ $\frac{1}{5}$	0.2
51%	$\frac{51}{100}$	0.51	72%	$\frac{72}{100}$ $\frac{18}{25}$	0.72
10%	$\frac{10}{100}$ $\frac{1}{10}$	0.1	33%	$\frac{33}{100}$	0.33
45%	$\frac{45}{100}$ $\frac{9}{20}$	0.45	49%	$\frac{49}{100}$	0.49
38%	$\frac{38}{100}$ $\frac{19}{50}$	0.38	36%	$\frac{36}{100}$ $\frac{9}{25}$	0.36

EXERCISE 12:4

1 18%	**2** 35%	**3** 55%	**4** 20%
5 70%	**6** 40%	**7** 8%	**8** 28%
9 10%	**10** 96%	**11** 65%	**12** 83%

EXERCISE 12:5

1 90%	**2** 55%	**3** 40%	**4** 65%
5 70%	**6** 35%	**7** 45%	**8** 20%

EXERCISE 12:6

1 28 m	**2** £45	**3** 21 km	**4** 512 g
5 £70	**6** 480 g	**7** 5.4 m	**8** 252

EXERCISE 12:7

1 £810	**2** 877.4 g	**3** 2400 m
4 76.5 kg	**5** £520	**6** £744
7 4.25 kg	**8** 1104 litres	

EXERCISE 12:8

1 28%	**2** 15%	**3** $2\frac{1}{2}$%
4 42%	**5** 31%	**6** 62%
7 8%	**8** English 65%; Maths 56%	

EXERCISE 12:9

1 $\frac{13}{40}$	**2** $\frac{7}{8}$	**3** $\frac{309}{400}$	**4** $\frac{19}{400}$
5 0.425	**6** 0.155	**7** 0.0825	**8** 0.0275
9 62.5%	**10** 5.5%	**11** 3.5%	**12** 44.5%
13 62.5%	**14** 31.25%	**15** £630	**16** £470
17 £175	**18** £170.10	**19** £82 800	**20** 23 500

ACTIVITY

Double your money

a

Year	1	2	3	4
Interest	£50	£52.50	£55.13	£57.88
Total	£1050	£1102.50	£1157.63	£1215.51

Year	5	6	7	8
Interest	£60.78	£63.81	£67.01	£70.36
Total	£1276.29	£1340.10	£1407.11	£1477.47

Year	9	10	11	12
Interest	£73.87	£77.57	£81.45	£85.52
Total	£1551.34	£1628.91	£1710.36	£1795.88

Year	13	14	15	
Interest	£89.79	£94.28	£99.00	
Total	£1885.67	£1979.95	£2078.95	

So it takes 15 years to double the money.

b If the interest rate falls to 4% then it takes 18 years to double £1000.

c Generally, the lower the interest rate, the longer it will take. The higher the interest rate, the shorter time it will take.

d For a starting amount of £2000 it will still take 15 years at 5% interest to double it.

e The amount of money you start with makes no difference to how long it takes to double the money.

Overall it is the interest rate, and not the amount of money you start with, that has a greater effect on the time it takes to double the money.

13 Measurement

This table shows how the sections in Chapter 13 in the *Number Works!* course book link to the sections in Chapter 13 of this homework book.

Course book section	2	3	4	5	6	7	8
Homework book section	1	2	3	4	5	6	7, 8

EXERCISE 13:1

1 2°C	**2** 6°C	**3** −5°C	**4** 7°C
5 −3°C	**6** −5°C	**7** 5°C	**8** 17°C

EXERCISE 13:2

1 18th February	**2** 1710
3 16th March	**4** 31 days
5 25th April	**6** Tuesday
7 15th July	**8** 57 days

EXERCISE 13:3

1 0725 h	**2** 2150 h	**3** 1010 h	**4** 2330 h
5 2.22 am	**6** 11.42 pm	**7** 10.50 am	**8** 1.04 pm
9 8.10 pm	**10** 0105 h		
11 1920 h	**12** 1.30 pm		

13	2 h 35 min	**14**	1 h 15 min
15	5 h 20 min	**16**	17 h 50 min

EXERCISE 13:4

1	5	**2**	2142	**3**	25 min
4	1827	**5**	38 min	**6**	2115
7	2127	**8**	1900, 2000		

EXERCISE 13:5

1	5 cm	**2**	7 cm	**3**	4.5 cm	**4**	6.5 cm
5	2.3 cm	**6**	5.8 cm	**7**	35 mm	**8**	55 mm
9	18 mm	**10**	28 mm	**11**	37 mm	**12**	60 mm
13	litres	**14**	g	**15**	m	**16**	mm
17	kg	**18**	cm				

EXERCISE 13:6

1	90 mm	**2**	0.055 g	**3**	600 cm	**4**	200 ml
5	38 000 m	**6**	1.7 litres	**7**	5.34 m	**8**	3.56 kg
9	800 kg	**10**	1900 g	**11**	50 ml	**12**	7 m
13	4	**14**	83	**15**	150 m		

EXERCISE 13:7

1	4 ft 2 in	**2**	21 ft	**3**	8 st 13 lb
4	35 oz	**5**	12 pt	**6**	8 oz
7	5 ft 10 in	**8**	4 pt	**9**	14 st 4 lb
10	39 in	**11**	51 oz	**12**	2 gal 6 pt
13	175 lb	**14**	78 in	**15**	60 fl oz
16	5 ft				

EXERCISE 13:8

1	30 cm	**2**	3½ m	**3**	66 lb	**4**	14 pt
5	120 cm	**6**	45 cm	**7**	9 litres	**8**	6 kg
9	1½ ft	**10**	16 km	**11**	32 litres	**12**	20 miles

ACTIVITIES

Hit the target

A game to practise working with negative numbers. You may use a calculator to check your answers.

14 Tables, graphs and charts

This table shows how the sections in Chapter 14 in the *Number Works!* course book link to the sections in Chapter 14 of this homework book.

Course book section	2	3	4	5	6	8	9
Homework book section	1	2	3, 4	5, 6	7	8	9

EXERCISE 14:1

1
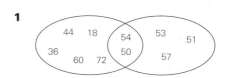

2

3
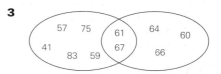

4
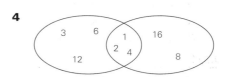

EXERCISE 14:2

1
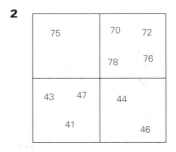

a	6	**b**	50, 52

2

a	75	**b**	6

3

33 55 11	22 88
37 53 19	62 24 48

a   5   **b**   19, 37, 53

EXERCISE 14:3

1

Shoe size	Tally	Frequency
3	///	3
4	~~HHT~~ ///	8
5	~~HHT~~ /	6
6	~~HHT~~ ///	8
7	///	3
8	//	2
	Total	30

2

Registration group	Tally	Frequency
A	~~HHT~~	5
E	~~HHT~~ /	6
L	~~HHT~~ ~~HHT~~	10
P	~~HHT~~	5
S	~~HHT~~ //	7
W	~~HHT~~ //	7
	Total	40

3

Fish caught	Tally	Frequency
1	///	3
2	////	4
3	~~HHT~~ //	7
4	~~HHT~~ ~~HHT~~	10
5	~~HHT~~ ////	9
6	~~HHT~~ //	7
	Total	40

EXERCISE 14:4

1

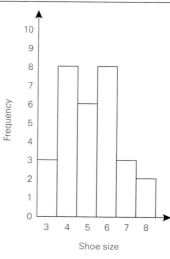

2

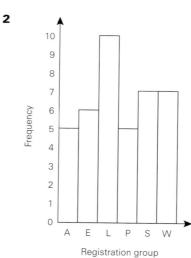

3

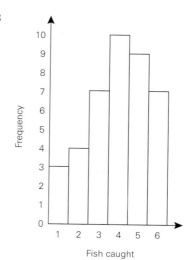

4

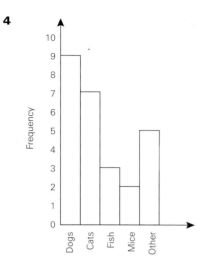

3

Amounts	Tally	Frequency
£0.00–£9.99	//	2
£10.00–£19.99	HHT ///	8
£20.00–£29.99	HHT	5
£30.00–£39.99	HHT //	7
£40.00–£49.99	HHT HHT	10
£50.00–£59.99	///	3
	Total	35

4

Marks	Tally	Frequency
21–30	//	2
31–40	//	2
41–50	////	4
51–60	HHT	9
61–70	HHT ////	9
71–80	HHT HHT	10
81–90	////	4
	Total	40

EXERCISE 14:5

1

Deliveries	Tally	Frequency
0–9	////	4
10–19	HHT //	7
20–29	HHT ///	8
30–39	HHT /	6
40–49	HHT	5
50–59	///	3
60–69	//	2
	Total	35

2

Marks	Tally	Frequency
0–9	///	3
10–19	HHT	5
20–29	HHT //	7
30–39	HHT ///	8
40–49	HHT /	6
50–59	////	4
60–69	//	2
	Total	35

EXERCISE 14:6

1

2

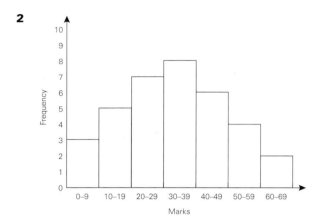

3

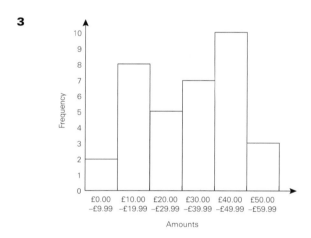

4

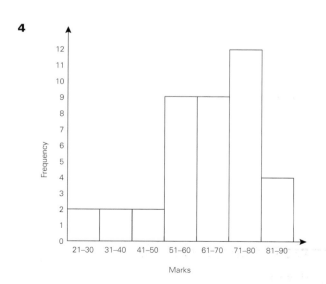

EXERCISE 14:7

1 a 30, 25   **b** Tuesday
   c Thursday $1\frac{1}{2}$ cars; Friday 2 cars
2 a 12, 13   **b** Usman
   c Bill: 4 fish; Roger $3\frac{1}{2}$ fish
3 a 16, 7   **b** 33
   c Thursday 5 tokens; Friday $2\frac{1}{4}$ tokens

EXERCISE 14:8

1 a 2   **b** 3   **c** 4,6
   d 18   **e** 35
2 a 9.2 m   **b** 8.7 m
   c 0900 h   **d** 2.2 m
3 a e   **b** 3   **c** 56
4 a 30   **b** Tuesday
   c Wednesday   **d** 75
5 a Thursday   **b** Monday
   c 3   **d** 39
6 a 83   **b** 1997
   c 19   **d** 169

EXERCISE 14:9

1 a green   **b** red and blue
   c i 10   **ii** 30
2 a mice   **b** dogs
   c i 10   **ii** 15
3 a cheese & onion
   b plain   **c** beef

ACTIVITIES

1 Survey of pets
Draw up an observation sheet that you can use to record your results. Or design a questionnaire you could ask people to fill in.

2 Fabfooty
The result is more likely to be a Home win, since this dice has more scores in it. The results in your table should show this to be the case.

Units of time

1 millennium = 1000 years
1 century = 100 years
1 decade = 10 years
1 year = 12 months = 52 weeks = 365 days
1 leap year = 366 days

A leap year occurs every **4** years: 1996, 2000, 2004, 2008, etc.

1 day = 24 hours   1 hour = 60 minutes
1 minute = 60 seconds
Midnight is 12 o'clock during the night
Midday is 12 o'clock during the day

Metric units

Length:
1 kilometre (km) = 1000 metres (m)
1 metre (m) = 100 centimetres (cm)
1 metre (m) = 1000 millimetres (mm)
1 centimetre (cm) = 10 millimetres (mm)

Weight:
1 kilogram (kg) = 1000 grams (g)
1 gram (g) = 1000 milligrams (mg)
1 tonne (t) = 1000 kilograms (kg)

Capacity:
1 litre (l) = 1000 millilitres (ml)

Imperial units

Length:
12 inches (in) = 1 foot (ft)
3 feet (ft) = 1 yard (yd)
1760 yards (yd) = 1 mile (m)

Weight:
16 ounces (oz) = 1 pound (lb)
14 pounds (lb) = 1 stone (st)

Capacity:
1 pint (pt) = 20 fluid ounces (fl oz)
8 pints (pt) = 1 gallon (gal)

Approximate metric and imperial equivalents

1 foot ≈ 30 centimetres
1 kg ≈ 2.2 pounds (weight)
1 km ≈ 5/8 mile

1 litre ≈ 1.75 pints
1 inch ≈ 2.5 centimetres
1 yard ≈ 1 metre

Adding table

+	1	2	3	4	5	6	7	8	9	10
1	2	3	4	5	6	7	8	9	10	11
2	3	4	5	6	7	8	9	10	11	12
3	4	5	6	7	8	9	10	11	12	13
4	5	6	7	8	9	10	11	12	13	14
5	6	7	8	9	10	11	12	13	14	15
6	7	8	9	10	11	12	13	14	15	16
7	8	9	10	11	12	13	14	15	16	17
8	9	10	11	12	13	14	15	16	17	18
9	10	11	12	13	14	15	16	17	18	19
10	11	12	13	14	15	16	17	18	19	20

Multiplication table

×	1	2	3	4	5	6	7	8	9	10
1	1	2	3	4	5	6	7	8	9	10
2	2	4	6	8	10	12	14	16	18	20
3	3	6	9	12	15	18	21	24	27	30
4	4	8	12	16	20	24	28	32	36	40
5	5	10	15	20	25	30	35	40	45	50
6	6	12	18	24	30	36	42	48	54	60
7	7	14	21	28	35	42	49	56	63	70
8	8	16	24	32	40	48	56	64	72	80
9	9	18	27	36	45	54	63	72	81	90
10	10	20	30	40	50	60	70	80	90	100